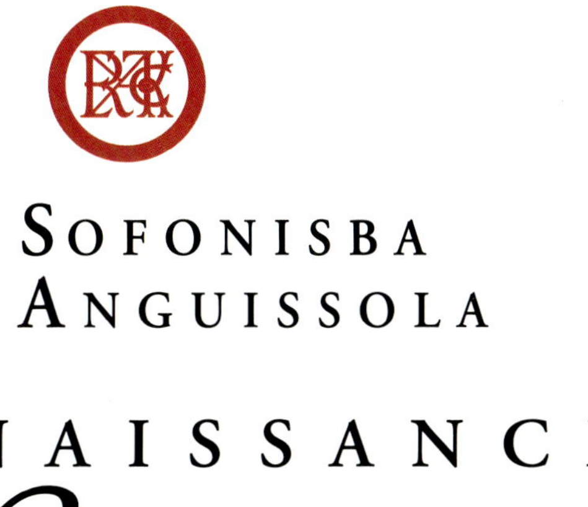
Sofonisba Anguissola
A Renaissance Woman

AF477406

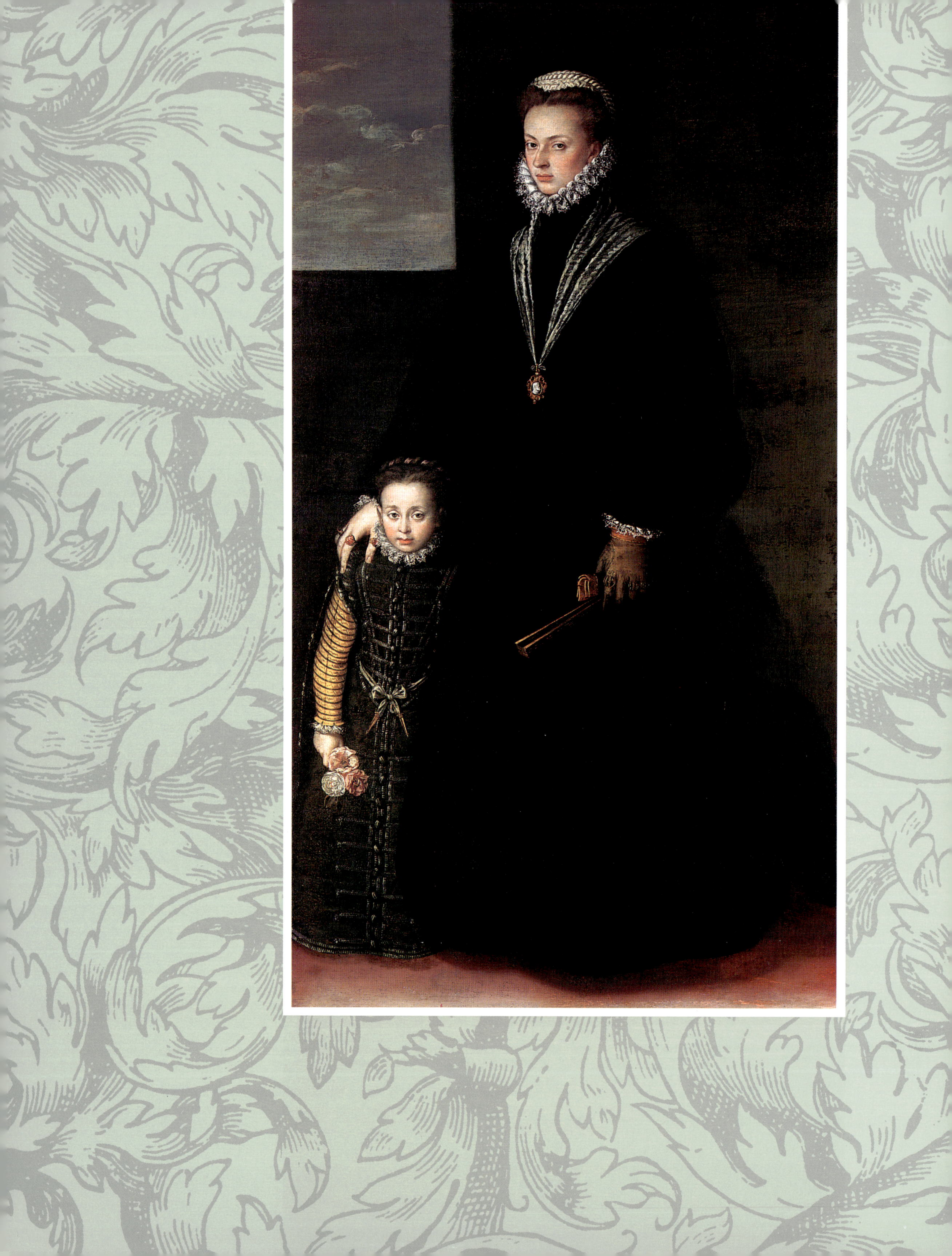

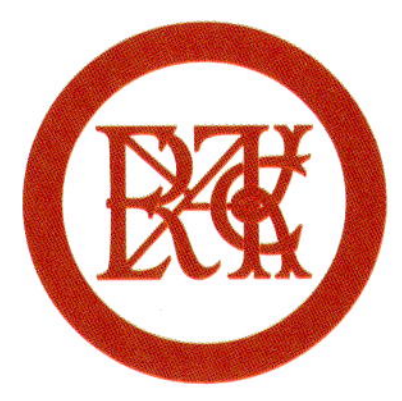

Sofonisba Anguissola
A Renaissance Woman

Sylvia Ferino-Pagden

Maria Kusche

The National Museum of Women in the Arts
Washington, D.C.
1995

This catalogue accompanies the exhibition *Sofonisba Anguissola: A Renaissance Woman* presented at The National Museum of Women in the Arts, Washington, D.C., from April 7 through June 15, 1995. The exhibition was drawn from the show *Sofonisba Anguissola e le sue sorelle*, organized by the Comitato Promotore Cremonese della Mostra Anguissola and displayed at Santa Maria della Pietà from September 14 through December 31, 1994. The Kunsthistoriches Museum in Vienna then presented the exhibition from January 17 through March 26, 1995.

TRANSLATED BY *Ulrike Mills and Eva Zimmerman*

EDITED BY *Brett Topping*

EDITORIAL ASSISTANCE BY *Jennifer Baggs*

DESIGNED BY *Dever Designs Inc., Laurel, Md.*

PRINTED BY *Virginia Lithograph, Arlington, Va.*

ISBN 0-940979-31-4

LIBRARY OF CONGRESS CATALOGING-IN-PUBLICATION DATA

Ferino Pagden, Sylvia.
Sofonisba Anguissola : a Renaissance woman / Sylvia Ferino-Pagden, Maria Kusche.
p. cm.
Exhibition catalog.
ISBN 0-940979-31-4
1. Anguissola, Sofonisba, ca. 1532-1625–Exhibitions.
2. Mannerism (Art)–Italy–Exhibitions. I. Anguissola, Sofonisba, ca. 1532 or 3-1625. II. Kusche, Maria. III. National Museum of Women in the Arts (U.S.) IV. Title.
ND623.A5395A4 1995 95-8170
759.5–dc20 CIP

COVER DETAIL

SOFONISBA ANGUISSOLA

Self-Portrait at the Easel

Oil on canvas, 26 x 22 1/2 in.

Lancut, Muzeum Zamek

FRONTISPIECE

ATTRIBUTED TO SOFONISBA ANGUISSOLA

Juana of Austria

Oil on canvas, 76 1/2 x 42 1/8 in.

Boston, Isabella Stewart Gardner Museum

CONTENTS

A C K N O W L E D G M E N T S

An exhibition such as this is necessarily the achievement of many dedicated individuals and organizations working together for a number of years. It will be impossible to recognize everyone whose efforts helped make this show possible. Among those who did are: members of Italy's diplomatic community, distinguished cultural institutions in the United States and around the world, the Comitato Promotore Cremonese della Mostra Anguissola and, of course, the lenders of the art works.

On behalf of the Board and staff of the museum, I extend special thanks to: His Excellency, The Ambassador of Italy and Mrs. Boris Biancheri for their unfailing support; Mr. Flavio Caroli, who first brought the idea of the exhibition to Mrs. Wilhelmina Cole Holladay, NMWA's Chairman of the Board, while serving as Cultural Attaché for the Embassy of Italy; Mr. Gian Carlo Corada, President of the Comitato Promotore Cremonese della Mostra Anguissola, and all the members of his dedicated committee; Ms. Mina Gregori, President of the Comitato Scientifico, and her distinguished committee members; Mr. Roberto Spinelli, Cultural Attaché, the Embassy of Italy; and Professor Margherita Ripetto, Director of the Italian Cultural Institute—along Ms. Melissa de Teffé, Senior Cultural Officer—for their sponsorship of education programs in connection with the exhibition.

Also deserving of distinct recognition are: Dr. Sylvia Ferino-Pagden, Curator of Italian Renaissance Art, Kunsthistorisches Museum, Vienna, who provided the introductory catalogue essay as well as invaluable assistance and advice in coordinating all aspects of this exhibition's continuation from Vienna to Washington; and Dr. Maria Kusche de Zettelmeyer whose years of scholarship on Sofonisba Anguissola are reflected in her catalogue essay for the Vienna catalogue, which she has generously granted us permission to reprint. A special word of thanks also goes to Mr. Claudio Ferri of Leonardo Arte in Milan for facilitating the production of NMWA's exhibition catalogue.

To those who kindly lent their art works to this most important exhibition, we extend our profound gratitude. They include: Pietro Petraroia, Soprintendente per i Beni Artistici e Storici di Milano; Antonio Paolucci, Soprintendente per i Beni Artistici e Storici delle province di Firenze e Pistoia; Aldo Cicinelli, Soprintendente per i Beni Artistici e Storici di

Brescia, Cremona e Mantova; Gary Vikan, Director, The Walters Art Gallery, Baltimore; Francesco Rossi, Director, Accademia Carrara, Bergamo; Malcom Rogers, Director, The Museum of Fine Arts, Boston; Renata Stradiotti, Director, Pinacoteca Tosio Martinengo, Brescia; Miklos Mojzer, Director, Szépmüvészeti Muzeum, Budapest; Brian Dursun, Director, The Lowe Art Museum, Coral Gables; Annamaria Petrioli Tofani, Director, Galleria degli Uffizi, Florence; The Duke of Richmond and Gordon, Goodwood Collection, Goodwood; Wit Woytowicz, Director, Muzeum Zamek, Lancut; Francisco Calvo Serraller, Director, Museo del Prado, Madrid; Pietro Petraroia, Director, Pinacoteca di Brera, Milan; Russell Bowman, Director, Milwaukee Art Museum; Konstanty Kalinowski, Director, Muzeum Narodowe, Poznán; Elizabeth Goodall, Director, Southampton City Art Gallery; and Karl Schütz, Director, Kunsthistorisches Museum, Vienna.

After a number of years and countless projects, I remain admiring of their skills and grateful for their dedication . . . staff members and interns whose contributions to this exhibition were enormous include: Susan Fisher Sterling, Edwin Penick, Randi Jean Greenberg, Tracy Fitzpatrick, Harriet McNamee, Brett Topping, Jennifer Baggs, Sally Anderson, Holly Crider, Mary Alice Nay, Jan Putnam and Nell Sutton.

Finally, I wish to thank Mr. Alessandro di Montezemolo for his constant dedication and unflagging optimism. It was a privilege and a great plesure to work with him on this extraordinary project.

Rebecca Anne Phillips Abbott

F O R E W O R D

A true pioneer of modernity, Sofonisba Anguissola is a fascinating and refined artist, capable of conveying great psychological intensity in her sitters–what da Vinci called the "motions of the soul." She was a painter who was famous in her day, then inexplicably forgotten. She has made a powerful comeback, however–from near total obscurity to being named "Woman of the Year" by a prominent Italian magazine. Clearly, she is an exemplary figure for our times.

From the outset the Comitato Promotore Cremonese della Mostra Anguissola (Committee to Promote the Anguissola Exhibition) wanted to bring Sofonisba back to Cremona–her paintings as well as her presence. In so doing, we sought not only to correct past oversights but to add significantly to our cultural knowledge. As a result, we have seen this exhibition as a great event as well as a kind of archaeological excavation of Renaissance society. We trust that we have left, in the process, precious materials for further investigations in the fields of art and history.

When the exhibition closed in Cremona, we felt sadness but great pride in our choice of two prestigious cultural institutions to serve as venues for the show–The Kunsthistorisches Museum in Vienna and The National Museum of Women in the Arts (NMWA) in Washington. It is satisfying to know that the cosmopolitan audiences served by these distinguished museums will come to know this noble Cremonese lady, the first in a long tradition of women artists. Our heartfelt thanks and recognition are owed to those responsible at NMWA, in particular Director Rebecca Phillips Abbott for embracing the exhibition. It has been reconceptualized with the same attentive diligence that originally inspired the Cremonese organizers.

Our collaboration with the museum has been meaningful because it advances knowledge and understanding between our cultures. In honoring Sofonisba, The National Museum of Women in the Arts honors Cremona, its citizens and all of Italy.

GIAN CARLO CORADA, President
Comitato Promotore Cremonese
della Mostra Anguissola
Cremona, Italy

MINA GREGORI, President
Comitato Scientifico Cremonese
della Mostra Anguissola
Cremona, Italy

Sylvia Ferino-Pagden

SOFONISBA ANGUISSOLA
The First Woman Painter

Without a doubt, Sofonisba Anguissola's greatest achievement was opening up painting to women as a socially acceptable profession. From the biography of Irene di Spilimbergo, a young lady highly educated in music and literature who died at an early age, we learn how much the example set by Sofonisba meant to her. When Irene saw one of Sofonisba's self-portraits, it awakened in her the desire not only to draw but to paint in oil, and to learn this from none other than Titian.[1] Artists' daughters as well surely were encouraged by her example to make a career as painters. In this they even may have received support from their parents, relatives and husbands, who hoped to gain fame and wealth from it.[2] This was the promise apparently provided by Sofonisba's example–that one could become recognized, respected and celebrated as a woman painter.

Painting as a profession also may have been ennobled by Sofonisba's personality and her social position. Although Boccaccio had already described artistic ability as a *nobilissima cosa*,[3] perhaps Sofonisba's great fame during her lifetime paved the way for future persons of noble rank to be able to devote themselves to the artistic profession.[4]

The status enjoyed by a woman artist, which varied from one period to another, was, thus, also a direct expression of a woman's general demeanor and the respect accorded her within the society of the day. This fact has already been demonstrated by numerous excellent studies on the sociohistorical preconditions for artistic activity by women throughout history.[5] In the field of painting, the earliest names of women painters which have come down to us, typically, are of the nuns who illuminated books. To give an idea of the ratio of men to women in this field, it may be noted that, out of approximately two thousand names of known miniature painters, about twenty are female.[6] Even the earliest women painters of large-format panels recorded by Giorgio Vasari frequently were nuns, such as Barbara Ragnoni or Plautilla Nelli, who worked in the 15th and 16th centuries, respectively.[7] It must be assumed, however, that not even these painting nuns were able to enjoy "professional" training, at that time only attained by men, and that their artistic production, of necessity, thus had to be quite modest.

Baldassare Castiglione, who represented the view that drawing and painting was part of a courtier's education, pointed out in this connection that in the ancient world, among Greeks and Romans, young men from the best families learned the fine arts and painting, but slaves were excluded from such studies.[8]

Castiglione's ideal courtier hardly would have received professional training, however, and would not have been able to measure up to the fully trained artist. In this respect the daughters of painters, who were allowed to participate in the work in their fathers' workshops, were privileged as the only women who had access to genuinely good training. These were also the women, such as Lavinia Fontana, Artemisia Gentileschi, Elisabetta Sirani and others, who would be the first to break through in this profession.

Artists' daughters had achieved a certain reputation with respect to their ability even before Sofonisba's time. Examples include Katharina van Hemessen,[9] the daughter of Jan Sanders van Hemessen, and Levina Teerlinc, daughter of Simon Benninck[10]—both of whom, by the way, also became court artists. Sofonisba, however, achieved her reputation as a professionally trained "dilettante" (in the sense of doing something for one's own delight rather than to earn money), and thus was celebrated as the first woman painter of the new era.

Sofonisba owed her training in painting to the wisdom of her ambitious father, Amilcare Anguissola, who, having had six daughters, was forced to adopt a plan that later turned out to be brilliant: to educate his daughters as he would male descendants. In so doing he provided them not only with a first-rate humanist education but even sent the two eldest girls, Sofonisba and Elena, to the workshop of the local master, Bernardino Campi, to teach them to paint professionally.

In doing this Amilcare also may have followed the previously mentioned trend of his day in accordance with which the women of the upper classes were given quite a prominent role. During the Renaissance, humanists began to acknowledge that women had other qualities beyond their importance as childbearers, even intellectual capabilities, and that they merited treatment that was more equal to that accorded to men. From the initial writings produced around 1480 on the "Defense of the Woman,"[11] there were soon "praises."[12] As the number of women who turned out to be worthy of these hymns of praise increased, written warnings to the men even appeared, stating they would soon be surpassed by the fine qualities of the women.[13]

While in Isabella d'Este's generation the humanist writers still passionately advocated equality for the woman, it may be concluded from the letters of the humanistically educated Partenia Gallerati from Cremona, who came from the same circles as Sofonisba, that women quickly became perfectly aware of their equal abilities. In a letter to her like-minded friend in Piedmont, Ginevra Scatileia di Cortemilia, Partenia urged that she support her female compatriots in their understanding that there should be as many intellectually trained women as men.[14]

The prelate and humanist Marco Gerolamo Vida from Cremona, a friend of Amilcare's, was demonstrably involved in launching the ladies of Cremona, first the poet and humanist Partenia Gallerati and then the young painter Sofonisba.[15] Amilcare's open, experimental education of his daughters and promotion of them becomes understandable, given this intellectual climate, in spite of the fact that he also hoped to obtain financial support through them. This latter goal actually came true in Sofonisba's case with the pension awarded her for life by the Spanish king.[16]

Naturally, Sofonisba herself contributed the most essential qualities to her success because she was intelligent, eager to learn and artistically talented. She also knew how to satisfy the demands imposed on her first by her father, then her teachers and later courtly society, fulfilling them beyond all expectations. Furthermore, she ultimately succeeded in determining and shaping her own life as a woman.

An early-maturing artist, Sofonisba initially was promoted by her father as a sensation, today one would say a child prodigy. She withstood these pressures due to her acquired advantages and innate virtues. While Vida had counted her among the most significant painters when she was only fifteen years old,[17] she soon became an "international" name due to the frequent letters produced by her manager-father. Michelangelo praised her; the humanist and art critic Annibale Caro requested a painting by her; princes and regents interested themselves in her works; even Vasari described her pictures in his *Vite de' più eccellenti pittori, scultori ed architettori.*[18] As late as the 17th and 18th century, collectors recognized her abilities and guarded her paintings as valuable treasures.

Toward the end of the 18th century, Sofonisba's fame disappeared, and in the 19th she was virtually forgotten. Her works were ascribed to male artists, such as Giovanni Battista Moroni and Titian. Although in documents and letters she is intertwined with the most important personalities of the first half of the 16th century, it was not until the turn of the 20th century that she began to achieve recognition again as an artist, based on her signed works. Subsequently, essays were devoted to her in art historical publications and the first book about her appeared in 1987.[19]

As the first woman painter to achieve fame and respect, Sofonisba was not in any professional competition with male artists. Nearly all of her pictures were produced as gifts and, thus, she did not take commissions away from other artists. As presents, these works—mostly self-portraits or portraits—circulated only in the most elevated circles. Therefore, they were not subjected to male art criticism, as were later works produced by the daughters of artists who followed in her footsteps. Vasari greatly admired the works he saw in her father's house, praising particularly their lifelike quality.[20]

Nevertheless, a quality-ranking of sorts, based on the subject of paintings, had become established in 16th-century art criticism, according to which the painter's supreme and most important task was the *storia,* as Leon Battista Alberti in the 15th century and Ludovico Dolce in the 16th century had already determined in their writings on art theory.[21] Portraiture thus acquired significantly less importance. According to Giovanni Battista Armenini, portrait painting even could be mastered by artists with mediocre talent, as long as they just were trained in coloring.[22] In his book on the artists working in Genoa written in 1674, Raffaello Soprani is the first to say in his discussion of Sofonisba that she, nevertheless, would have been quite good at creating *storie* and *invenzioni,* and that is was not for lack of talent that she painted so few of them, for she already had proven this in works such as *The Chess Game.* According to Soprani, she was so swamped with portrait commissions, however, that she had no time for more important subjects.[23] Carlo

Malvasia, on the other hand, mentioned her only by name as a portrait painter, together with Lavinia Fontana and Fede Galizia.[24]

Thus, while the nearly contemporary art critics spared Sofonisba, they dealt considerably less favorably with the professional daughters of artists. Since, just as with their male competitors, they were dependent on commissions and had to make a living from their profession, very soon all the male prejudices were heaped on them. Some were completely passed over in silence, as was the case with Artemisia Gentileschi, who was ignored by the art critics of her day. Important 17th-century art critics and theoreticians, such as Giovanni Battista Passeri or Giovanni Baglione, had little fear of downgrading art by such painters as Lavinia Fontana or Caterina Ginnasi as women's work. In general, evaluations of paintings done by women published in 17th-century works almost uniformly contain the deprecatory limitation—perhaps quite good for a work by a woman.[25] In this respect nothing had changed since Boccaccio, who, with the help of Pliny, praised a group of women artists all the more, since he had to take into account, after all, how foreign art was to women and how little talent they generally possessed.[26]

This type of prejudice endured through centuries, even if individual female artists achieved a position in history. Some of the women who succeeded in the 17th century include still life and genre painters Clara Peeters and Judith Leyster; among the successful 18th- century painters are the pastel artist Rosalba Carriera, the French society portraitist Elisabeth Vigée-Lebrun and Angelica Kauffman, who painted classical myths.[27]

The prejudices against which women struggled culminated in the 19th century. This was a time in which women had to endure the burden of hypercritical moral constraints of a society wavering in its foundations and during which they were being excluded from public instruction at universities, academies and all forms of higher professional training.[28]

With the beginning of our century, however, women united and fought for their rights. The first organizations of women artists were aimed at realizing the possibilities of a specialized education and a professional career. More recently, since the 1970s, women have begun systematically exploring their own history, which also includes that of women artists of the past. It is thanks to American women historians, in particular, that these once famous female ancestors, among them women artists, again are being saved gradually from oblivion or neglect.

The first great exhibition on famous women painters of five centuries arranged by Ann Sutherland Harris and Linda Nochlin in 1976 in Los Angeles, *Women Artists 1550-1950*, initiated a series of other exhibitions organized in America and Europe. These presentations encouraged contemporary women artists, while stimulating interest in monographic exhibitions of the women painters of the past. An exhibition in 1991 at Casa Buonarroti in Florence devoted to Artemisia Gentileschi brought to light this exceptional woman painter of the Baroque. Judith Leyster was celebrated in 1993 at the Frans

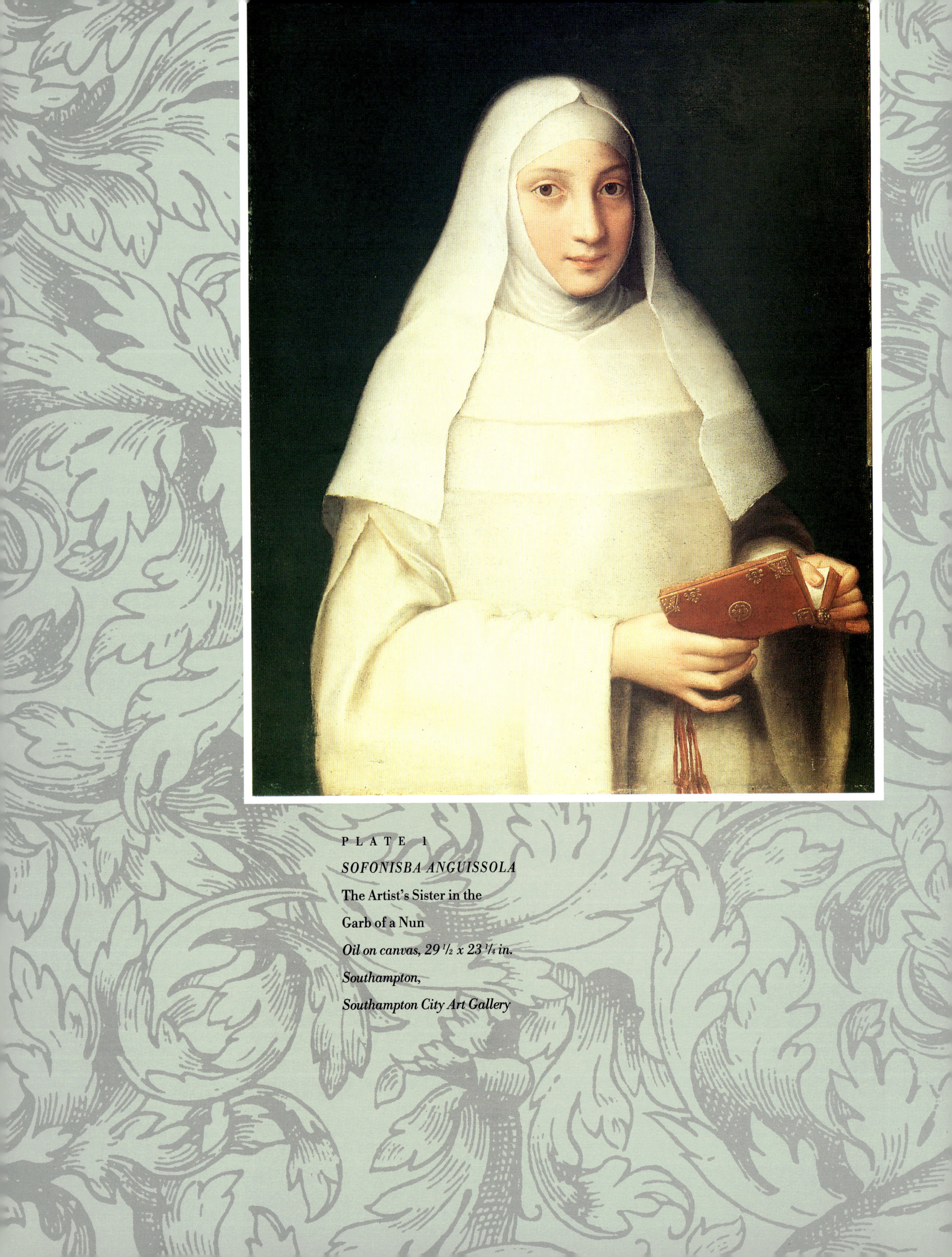

PLATE 1

SOFONISBA ANGUISSOLA

The Artist's Sister in the Garb of a Nun

Oil on canvas, 29 1/2 x 23 1/4 in.

Southampton, Southampton City Art Gallery

P L A T E ◆ 1

This portrait, which first appears in the collection of Lord Yarborough in London in 1854, was thought to be by Titian in the 19th century. The attribution was corrected after an inscription, now no longer legible, was found on the verso of the painting: *Sophonisba Angussola Virgo M...teri Ago.ti Pinxit MDLI.* The inscription also led to the hypothetical identification of the subject as Elena Anguissola, the only nun among Sofonisba's sisters (Wey 1861, cited by F. Sacchi 1872, 6, VI). Elena had been a student of Bernardino Campi as well, and then entered the Dominican convent of San Vincenzo in Mantua to become a nun (regarding Elena, see Gilardi in exh. cat. Cremona 1994, 75).

Another interpretation of the fragmentary inscription as *Monasteri (Sancti) Agostini(?)* (Caroli 1987, 92) may indicate that the subject was a novice of the Augustine order (whose habit was also white), but rules out the identification as Elena Anguissola, who was a Dominican. The identification of the subject as Elena, here about fourteen or fifteen years old, is the most plausible solution because of her family resemblance. The facial features correspond with another portrait that is assumed to be of Elena Anguissola, the *Dominican Nun as Saint Catherine*, at the Galleria Borghese (Rome).

With its date of 1551, the portrait in Southampton is the earliest extant work by Sofonisba, and must have been produced during her apprenticeship with Bernardino Gatti. The natural, lively, immediately engaging appearance of this subject makes her personable; she appears to be accessible and lifelike. The close attention paid to the observation of nature, expressed in the way the subject's fingers hold the book, with its red, gold-decorated leather cover, has been addressed by M. C. Rodeschini Galati (1990) as a typically Lombard element stemming from Sofonisba's teachers.

Exh. cat. Cremona 1994, no. 1 (R. Sacchi)

—*ALEXANDER WIED*

P L A T E ◆ 2

According to the latest research, Sofonisba was only fifteen years old when she was listed by the famous Cremonese bishop and humanist Marco Gerolamo Vida as *inter egregios pictores nostri temporis* (Gregori in exh. cat. Cremona 1994, 11). This small picture, which is dated 1554, is today thought to be her earliest extant self-portrait. Despite its small format, Sofonisba's goal of making her mark in history as a painter is already fully apparent here. She is looking at the viewer from the left, with large, serious eyes. Her hair is austerely parted, pulled back and fastened on her head, and she is dressed in a simple black doublet, perhaps a painter's frock, which she wears over a shirt and a dress with blackberry-colored sleeves. Somber, without jewelry, she presents herself in front of a neutral green background, not as a young noblewoman but as a humanistically educated young woman with an open book. Expressis verbis she introduces herself as virgo, a maiden—a conscious reference to the famous woman painter from antiquity called Iaia by Pliny and Marcia by Boccaccio. Both called her a *perpetua virgo,* who neither served the Vesta nor any other priestess but renounced physical pleasure to dedicate herself fully to the arts (Schweikart 1992, 115; Ghirardi in exh. cat. Bologna 1994, 39).

Like most of Sofonisba's surprisingly prodigious number of self-portraits, this one also may have been intended as a token for an admirer. Sofonisba's social status did not allow her to sell works of art. They were most often intended as gifts for friends who valued her artistic capabilities.

This portrait probably is identifiable with the one described by Sofonisba's father, Amilcare Anguissola, in a letter of 1556, which was intended as a present for Duke Ercole d'Este II. Together with other paintings, it may have been sent by Cardinal d'Este to Emperor Rudolph II in 1603/04.

Exh. cat. Cremona 1994, no. 2 (R. Sacchi)

—*SYLVIA FERINO-PAGDEN*

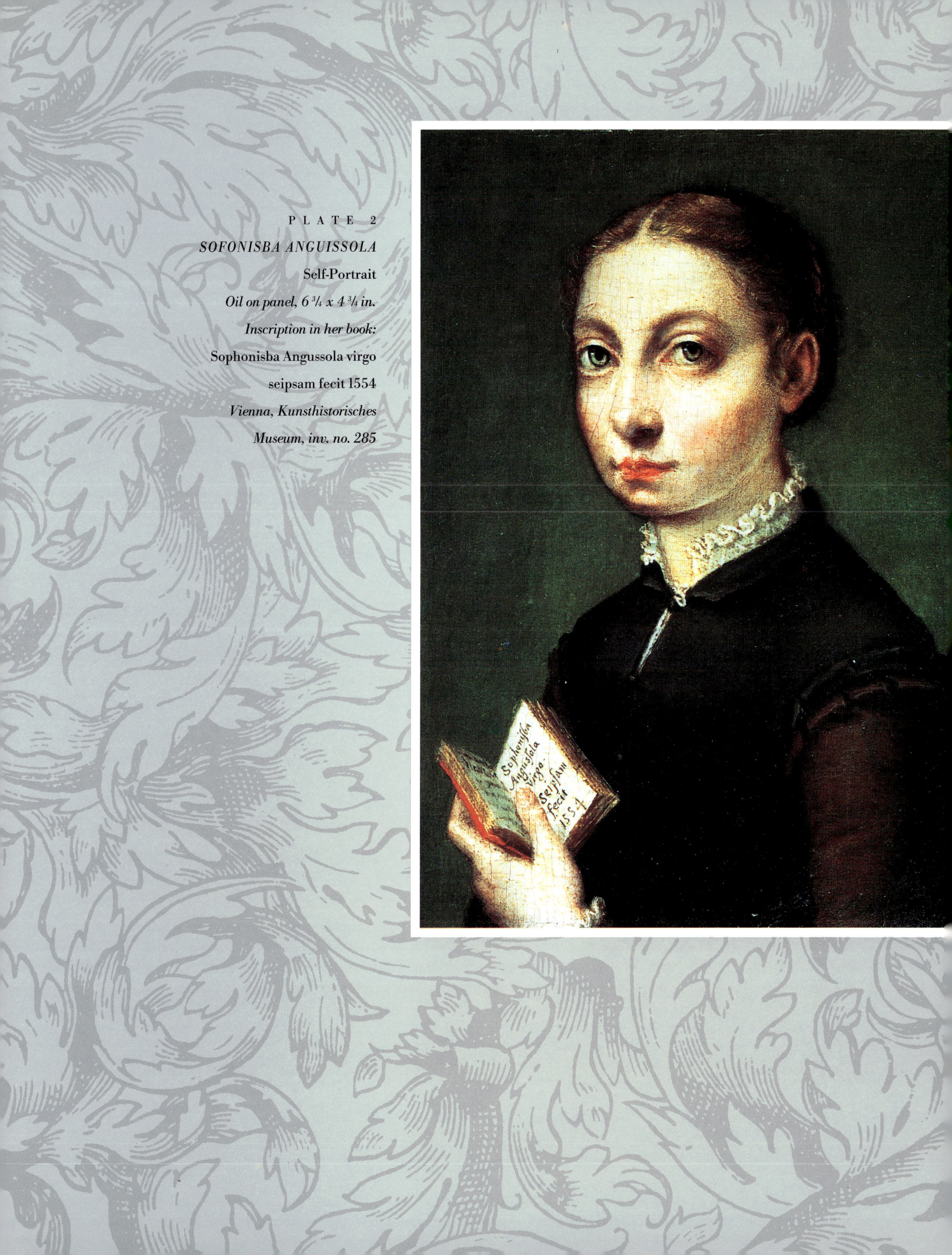

PLATE 2

SOFONISBA ANGUISSOLA

Self-Portrait

Oil on panel, 6 ¾ x 4 ¾ in.

Inscription in her book:

Sophonisba Angussola virgo

seipsam fecit 1554

Vienna, Kunsthistorisches

Museum, inv. no. 285

Hals Museum in Haarlem, at the Worcester Art Museum in Worcester, Massachusetts, and in a focus exhibition at The National Museum of Women in the Arts in Washington.[29] The two most famous women painters of the 16th century, Sofonisba Anguissola and Lavinia Fontana, finally were honored for the first time in 1994 by monographic exhibitions organized in Cremona and Bologna.[30]

It is perhaps precisely today that the major reputation Sofonisba enjoyed during her lifetime is being critically analyzed by art historians and art critics for the first time, in light of her works that have been assembled only now. Her talent is also being reassessed, in comparison to that of the women painters who followed her. Compared with the artistic ability demonstrated by the works of artists such as Artemisia Gentileschi, for example, it is said that Sofonisba's fame as a painter is not really justified. Her subject matter is limited primarily to portrait and genre scenes that are always of the family. Her few paintings of a devotional nature, which are derived from other masters' compositions, hardly show any creative attributes. In fact, it is said, Sofonisba's work lacks dramatic representations, such as those found later in the 17th-century paintings of Artemisia Gentileschi. Sofonisba actually demonstrated little interest in depicting *storia* (history or narrative) in Leon Battista Alberti's sense, or in developing the artistic skill necessary to compose it.

There are other difficulties as well. For example, her works do not lend themselves to chronological dating in accordance with art historical custom, which may be seen as confirming her "dilettantism." There is, in fact, a certain amount of difficulty in dating Sofonisba's paintings on the basis of the principles of stylistic development, which, incidentally, causes a great deal of trouble for the scholar of portrait painting in general.

Yet these dating criteria which are so essential to the art historian are the result of an unbroken male artistic tradition which, by definition, cannot be relevant to women, since, until recently, they have not had access to that tradition. Although Sofonisba may have been a sensation as woman painter in her own time, it remains clear that she, just as the women artists who followed her—Lavinia Fontana, Artemisia Gentileschi and many others—undoubtedly were not the female equivalents of Michelangelo, Titian or Raphael, nor of Moretto or Moroni, Carracci or Poussin. This must not inevitably lead to the conclusion that women are fundamentally less artistically talented than men, however, although that has been the usual opinion of literati and art critics from Boccaccio to the present century, as discussed by Linda Nochlin in her groundbreaking essay "Why Have There Been No Great Women Artists?" Nochlin pointed out that women painters simply were not able to rely on the same unbroken tradition as men, and for that reason did not develop talents comparable to theirs.[31] This essay proves that artistic talent and genius could only grow from the uninterrupted fertile ground of hands-on practice and its intellectual preconditions.

Perhaps one should, therefore, take another look at Sofonisba's artistic creations, and even at the critiques of her work. Regarding the objection to her limited subject matter, Soprani supplied a plausible explanation as early as the 17th century. As a painting noblewoman Sofonisba, in contrast to nearly all other Italian women artists recorded in history well into the 18th century, was not the daughter of a painter. In addition to the fact that she was not able to learn dramatic design or complex compositions adequately from her teacher Bernardino Campi, who was just as unremarkable in this area as she, decisions also surely were made from the outset about the fields in which she would be trained. These were primarily themes which she was able to realize in her home and family environment, meaning studies from nature and the portrait. In executing these subjects she was able to bring to bear both her education and intellectual background, while demonstrating the qualities society expected from a woman: virtue, chastity and humility.

In her self-portraits she appears highly determined, constrained and serious, unadorned and stern, whether with a book (plate 2), holding a shield (plate 3), in front of the easel (plate 4) or at the spinet (plate 5). She always has a very impressive gaze, however, in which humility and self-confidence combine in a strange mixture forming a distinctive artistic-professional self-image. The courage to represent herself unembellished in a manner that asks to be taken seriously, yet with a level of artistry which hardly appears inferior to that of her teachers, Bernardino Campi and Bernardino Gatti, was by no means a matter of course for a female, or a male, painter of the day. The qualities these self-portraits reveal also may have aided her intellectual development into a young, humanistically educated yet professionally trained painter. In this respect her knowledge of the famous women painters of the ancient world, as first described by Pliny and later given special attention by Boccaccio, must have been a source of major support.[32] As Gunter Schweikhart pointed out, she obviously refers to them when she characterizes herself in the self-portraits as a *virgo* and, in so doing, stresses that she made a mirror image of herself.[33] In other self-portraits, for instance when she is in the act of painting an image of the Madonna on the easel, she shows that she is aware of the tradition available to a woman painter by referring to Boccaccio's Thamar.[34] She also brings her intellect to bear when she paints her sisters in *The Chess Game* (plate 6), which is an altogether proper activity for young women, or in *The Family Portrait* (Nivaa, Nivaagaards Malerisamling). In the latter, even with an open-air setting, she clearly knows how to integrate the iconographically intricate curtain motif. The most demanding picture from the aspect of art theory, however, is her double picture in Sienna (Pinacoteca Nazionale), in which she shows herself being painted by Bernardino Campi.

The tremendous leap from the intimate family themes of her Cremona period to the official court portraits produced during her fourteen-year stay in Spain, which thanks to Maria Kusche's intensive studies has now become comprehensible, is clearly evident in her extremely high-quality images of the royal family. These works, impressive in their form as well as color, ultimately prove her artistic abilities and justify her international reputation. Nevertheless, as Maria Kusche has put forth so beautifully, Sofonisba knew how to concentrate on the human qualities in these courtly portraits of the Spanish and Genoese period, despite the limitations imposed by the court ceremonial, and express her subjects' individuality and warmth.[35]

Even if we accept that Sofonisba was not a major historical painter, she nevertheless pioneered the "genre" theme for Italy, for which the artist and art theorist Giovanni Paolo Lomazzo from Lombardy praised her.[36] Through her gift of observing nature she opened up a new field of the "comical" in art. Her inventions, such as that of her brother pinched by the crab in his sister's presence (Naples, Museo di Capodimonte) or the old woman who is learning the alphabet to the humorous delight of a girl (Florence, Galleria degli Uffizi), are truly *invenzioni*, as Tommaso Cavalieri wrote to Duke Cosimo I de' Medici,[37] and, in Soprani's words, even *capricci.*[38] In the paintings of her family members and friends, she always penetrates deeper into the psyche of those depicted and tells us something new about the person, although perhaps with less brilliant portrait composition. From what other 16th-century painting in Italy has a little girl ever laughed out at us so directly and happily as little Europa does in *The Chess Game?* It is these quite gentle, soft, psychologically far-reaching tones which give Sofonisba Anguissola's art its special quality.

NOTES

1. Valerio Guazzoni, "Donna, pittrice e gentildonna. La nascita di un mito femminile del Cinquecento," *Sofonisba Anguissola e le sue sorelle*, exhibition catalogue, ed. Paolo Buffa (Cremona: Leonardo Arte, 1994), 65.

2. See A. Ghirardi, "Lavinia Fontana allo specchio: Pittrici e autoritratto nel secondo Cinquecento," *Lavinia Fontana 1552-1614*, exhibition catalogue (Milan, 1994), 37ff.

3. Adriano Prandi, "Giovanni Boccaccio e l'arte Figurativa," *Bulletin de l'Institut Historique Belge de Rome* (1976-77): 101-51. See particularly, 111.

4. Alessandro Lamo, *Discorso intorno alla scoltura et pittura* (Cremona, 1584), 37-44. See, Rossana Sacchi, "Fonti a stampa e letterarie 1550-1625," in *Sofonisba Anguissola e le sue sorelle* (Cremona: Leonardo Arte, 1994), 407.

5. For a sociohistoric overview on the situation of women artists, I recommend these publications, to name a few. Ann Sutherland Harris and Linda Nochlin, *Women Artists 1550-1950*, exhibition catalogue (Los Angeles: Los Angeles County Art Museum, 1976); Linda Nochlin, *Women, Art, and Power* (New York: Harper & Row, 1988); Whitney Chadwick, *Women, Art, and Society* (New York, Thames and Hudson, 1990).

6. Harris and Nochlin, *Women Artists*, footnote 24.

7. Harris and Nochlin, *Women Artists*, 20-21.

8. Baldassare Castiglione, *Il cortegiano* (1528), 1:49.

9. Harris and Nochlin, *Women Artists*, 105. See also, *Sofonisba Anguissola e le sue sorelle* (Cremona: Leonardo Arte, 1994), cat. no. 66.

10. Harris and Nochlin, *Women Artists*, 102-04.

11. Maria Kusche, "Sofonisba Anguissola: Leben und Werk," *Sofonisba Anguissola*, exhibition catalogue, ed. Sylvia Ferino-Pagden (Vienna, Kunsthistorisches Museum, 1995), 24f. See also C. Fahy, "Three Early Treatises on Women," *Italian Studies* 11 (1956): 30-55.

12. Guazzoni, "Donna, pittrice e gentildonna," 57ff.

13. Guazzoni, "Donna, pittrice e gentildonna," 58, cites Ortensio Landi as stating, "Essortatione a gli huomini perché non si lascino superar dalle donne." Compare C. Fahy, *Italian Studies* 138 (1961): 154-272.

14. Guazzoni, "Donna, pittrice e gentildonna," 59, 61.

15. Guazzoni, "Donna, pittrice e gentildonna," 59f, and *Sofonisba Anguissola*, (Vienna, Kunsthistorisches Museum, 1995), cat. no. 86.

16. See Kusche, "Sofonisba Anguissola: Leben und Werk," and cat. nos. 95-97, in *Sofonisba Anguissola* (Vienna, Kunsthistorisches Museum, 1995).

17. Marco Gerolamo Vida, *Cremonensium Orationes III adversus Papienses in controversia Principatus* (1550), 64 vol.

18. Mina Gregori, "Fama e oblio di Sofonisba Anguissola," *Sofonisba Anguissola e le sue sorelle* (Cremona: Leonardo Arte, 1994), 1ff.

19. Flavio Caroli, *Sofonisba Anguissola e le sue sorelle* (Milan: A. Mondadori, 1987).

20. G. Milanesi, ed., *Le opere di Giorgio Vasari* (Florence, 1878-85), 6:498f.

21. Leon Battista Alberti *Della pittura* (1540), trans. John R. Spencer (Westport: Greenwood Press, 1976), 60. Lodovico Dolce, *Dialogo della pittura intitolato l'Aretino* (1557), trans. W. Brown (1770; reprint, New York: M. W. Roskill, 1968), 85ff.

22. Giovanni Battista Armenini, *De' veri precetti della pittura* (1587), trans. Edward J. Olszewski (New York: B. Franklin, 1977), 3, 11, 190. See also Fredrika H. Jacobs, "Women's Capacity to Create: The Unusual Case of Sofonisba Anguissola," *Renaissance Quarterly* 47, no. 1 (Spring 1994): 74-101.

23. Raffaele Soprani, *Vite de' pittori, scultori, ed architetti genovesi* (1674; reprint, Genoa: Stamperia Casamara, 1768-69), 413.

24. Carlo Cesare Malvasia, *Felsina pittrice: Vite dei pittori bolognesi* (1678; reprint, Bologna: Tip Guidi All'ancora, 1841) 2: 9, 97.

25. Harris and Nochlin, *Women Artists*, 31.

26. Harris and Nochlin, *Women Artists*, 23. For further examples see Giacomo Manzoni, *Della donne famose di Giovanni Boccaccio* (Bologna: Presso G. Romagnoli, 1881), 181; and Adriano Prandi, "Giovanni Boccaccio e l'arte figurativa," *Bulletin de l'Institut historique Belge de Rome* 46-47 (1976-77): 101-51.

27. Harris and Nochlin, *Women Artists*, 32-44.

28. Harris and Nochlin, *Women Artists*, 45ff; Sabine Plankolm-Forsthuber, *Künstlerinnen in Österreich 1887-1938* (Vienna, 1994), 39ff.

29. Roberto Contini and Gianni Papi, *Artemisia*, exhibition catalogue (Rome: Leonardo, 1991). James A. Welu and Pieter Biesboer, *Judith Leyster: A Dutch Master and Her World*, exhibition catalogue (Worcester, Mass.: Worcester Art Museum, 1993).

30. *Sofonisba Anguissola e le sue sorelle*, ed. Paolo Buffa (Cremona: Leonardo Arte, 1994). V. Fortunati, *Lavinia Fontana 1552-1614*, exhibition catalogue (Milan, 1994).

31. Linda Nochlin, *Women, Art, and Power*, 149f.

32. Gunter Schweikart, "Boccaccios, 'De claris mulierbus' und die Selbstdarstellung von Malerinnen im 16. Jahrhundert," in *Der Künstler über sich selbst in seinem Werk* (1989), 117ff.

33 Schweikart, "Boccaccios," 119ff.

34. Schweikhart, "Boccaccios," 123f.

35. See Maria Kusche's essay in this catalogue, as well as those in the Cremona and Vienna catalogues cited above.

36. Giovanni Paolo Lomazzo, *Scritti sulle arti* (1584; reprint, Florence: Marchi & Bertolli, 1974), 2:315.

37. *Sofonisba Anguissola e le sue sorelle* (Cremona: Leonardo Arte, 1994), 370.

38. Soprani, *Vite de' pittori*, 412.

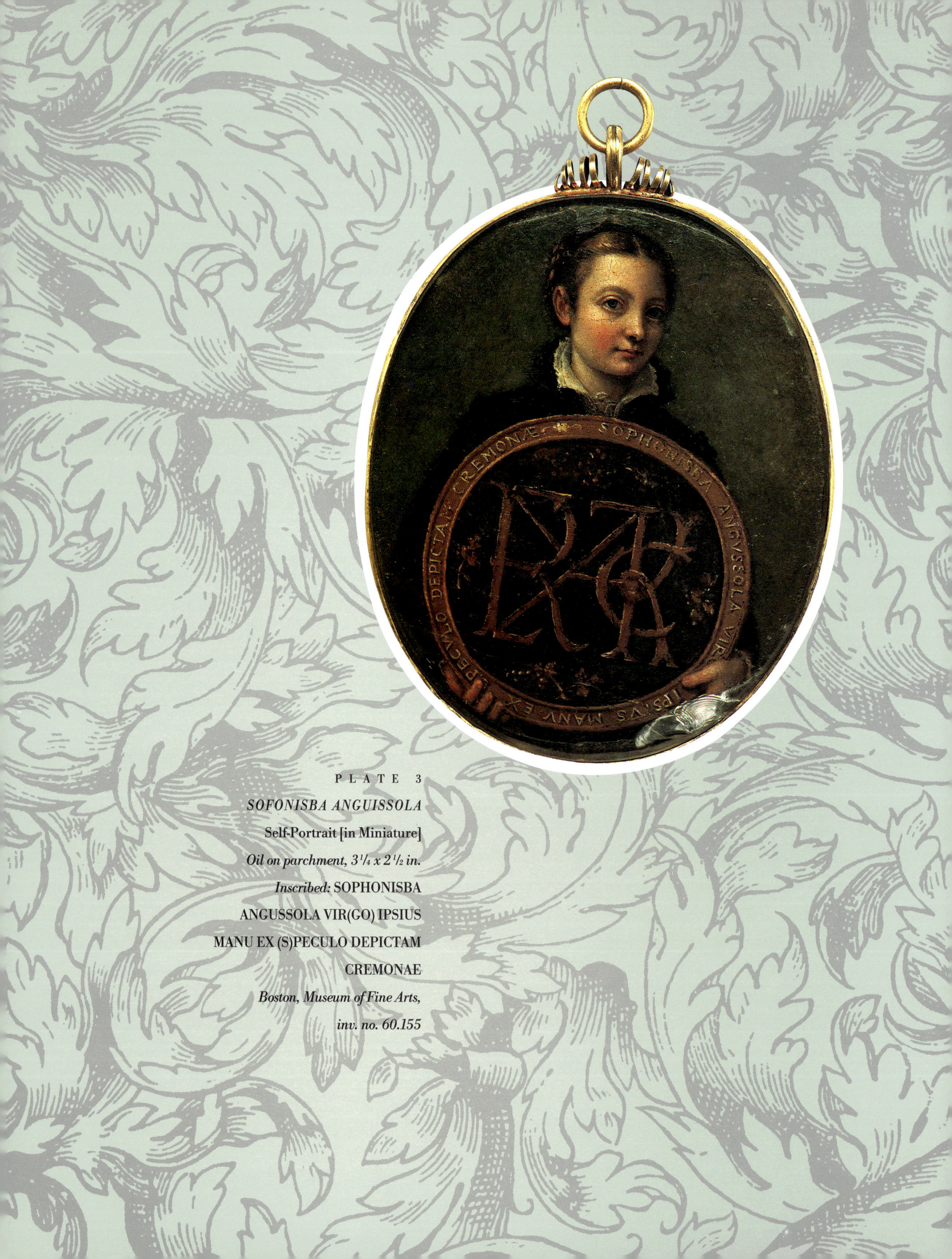

PLATE 3

SOFONISBA ANGUISSOLA

Self-Portrait [in Miniature]

Oil on parchment, 3 1/4 x 2 1/2 in.

Inscribed: SOPHONISBA ANGUSSOLA VIR(GO) IPSIUS MANU EX (S)PECULO DEPICTAM CREMONAE

Boston, Museum of Fine Arts, inv. no. 60.155

PLATE • 3

The lack of ornamentation, the severe dress and the green background, as well as Sofonisba's approximate age, are almost identical with the Vienna self-portrait. The explicitly chosen miniature format and the use of parchment as painting support may indicate the influence of miniature painter Giulio Clovio, then a very famous artist who was also portrayed by Sofonisba (plate 9). A most unusual feature of this oval, gold-mounted self-portrait is the large disk that Sofonisba holds with both hands before her upper torso.

The center of this shield is filled with mysterious initials. An inscription around the outside of the medallion explains that Sofonisba painted her portrait with the help of a mirror, as her famous predecessor from antiquity had done, a painter referred to as Iaia by Pliny and Marcia by Boccaccio. The entwined initials perhaps can be deciphered as AMILCARE (the name of Sofonisba's father), which would, however, not account for the K (on the right). The shield reminds Schweikhart (1992, 120) of representations of Prudentia, who had a mirror as one of her attributes and was represented in late Medieval manuscripts with similarly inscribed shields. Sofonisba may have wanted to allude to an aspect of virtue that she herself strove to attain. This is all the more likely, since the mirror also carried negative connotations, especially that of vanity.

Such a tiny work of art might at first seem designed as a personal present for relatives, but the designation CREMONAE suggests instead that an outside recipient was intended for this precious gift.

Exh. cat. Cremona 1994, no. 6 (R. Sacchi)

—*SYLVIA FERINO-PAGDEN*

P L A T E • 4

Newly discovered during preparations for the exhibition in Cremona, this painting is a valuable addition to the artist's oeuvre. The portrait, perhaps because of its fluid brushwork, is dated somewhat earlier (around 1556) than the *Self-Portrait at the Spinet* in Naples (Museo di Capodimonte), which is very similar in style and composition. Compared to the portrait from Naples, Sofonisba presents herself here in more formal fashion and more acutely observed. Perhaps she wanted to alert the viewer, with her own closer observation of nature, to the demands for concentration that her calling as an artist required. Interrupted in her work on a painting of the Madonna, she turns to the viewer with her characteristically serious, yet open, almost inquisitive look.

Women artists had been portrayed at the easel painting self-portraits before Sofonisba. In the early 15th-century illustrations for Boccaccio's work *De claris mulieribus*, the painter Marcia is shown creating her own portrait with the help of a mirror (Schweikhart 1992, ill., 7, 8). Sofonisba herself had made an earlier self-portrait at the easel (exh. cat. Cremona 1994, 67), which is especially close in its composition to a self-portrait by Caterina van Hemessen that dates back to 1548 (Kunstmuseum, Basel, inv. no. 361, exh. cat. Cremona 1994, 66). She later produced additional versions, as shown, for example, by the copy in the Zeri Collection in Mentana (exh. cat. Cremona 1994, no. 8). In all these self-portraits Sofonisba is always at work on the same painting of the Madonna, who conspicuously and tenderly hugs her child nestled closely against her. Perhaps this picture of the Madonna really existed. As a painter of Madonna portraits Sofonisba also may have identified with her mythical predecessor Timarete, or Thamar, who, according to Pliny, had created a painting of Diana of Ephesus and, according to Boccaccio, also a famous work depicting the Madonna. Sofonisba also presents herself here as the female counterpart to the Evangelist Luke, who was the archetypal Madonna painter or Christian artist (Ghirardi in exh. cat. Bologna 1994, 41).

Exh. cat. Cremona 1994, no. 7 (R. Sacchi)

—SYLVIA FERINO-PAGDEN

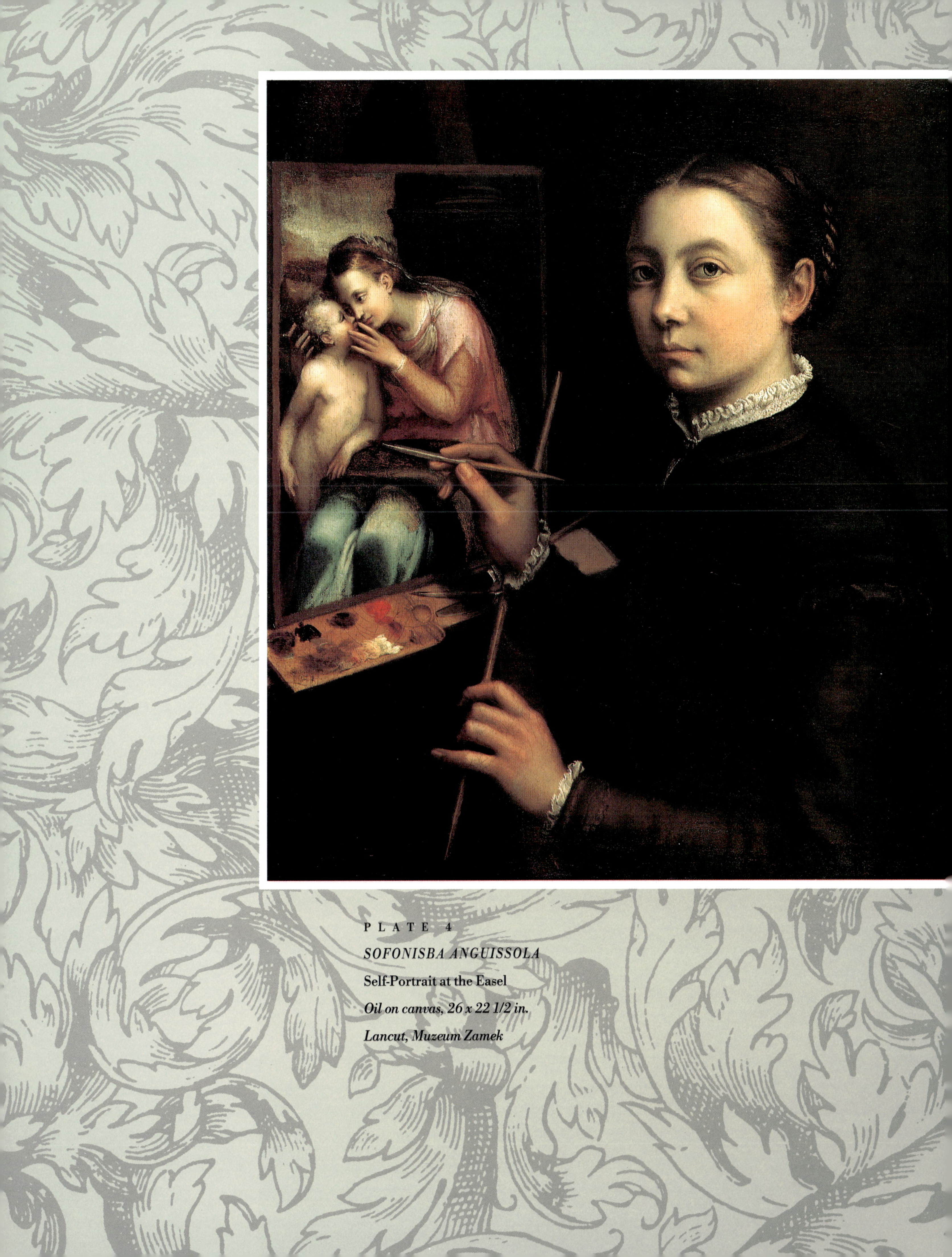

PLATE 4

SOFONISBA ANGUISSOLA

Self-Portrait at the Easel

Oil on canvas, 26 x 22 1/2 in.

Lancut, Muzeum Zamek

MARIA KUSCHE

SOFONISBA ANGUISSOLA

Her Life and Work

Nostros vivimos en esa casa movediza del tiempo; sin embargo, la historia detiene sus figuras, porque en ella nunca se dice adiós del todo, lo que una vez sucede se queda sucediendo para siempre.—ANTONIO GALA

In this essay new data and pictorial material, as well as new research results, published in the exhibition catalogue Sofonisba Anguissola e le sue sorelle *(Cremona: Leonardo Arte, 1994) are combined into a first comprehensive overview of the painter's life and work. The essay is based on the following articles in that catalogue.*

For Sofonisba's life in Italy—her time in Cremona, Palermo, Genoa and again in Palermo—I have used the articles and documents of Rossana Sacchi, "Tra la Sicilia e Genova: Sofonisba Anguissola Moncada e poi Lomellini"; "Intorno agli Anguissola"; "Regesto dei documenti"; and "Fonti a stampa e letterarie 1550-1625." For Sofonisba's education in Cremona I have drawn, in part, on Giulio Bora, "Sofonisba Anguissola e la sua formazione cremonese: Il ruolo del disegno." As for the role of women in Sofonisba's time and in her circle, I have relied on Valerio Guazzoni, "Donna, pittrice e gentildonna: La nascita di un mito femminile del Cinquecento." Regarding her sisters I have referred to Anastasia Gilardi, "Le sorelle di Sofonisba." For Sofonisba's life in Spain and her further contacts with Spain after returning to Italy, my own essay "Sofonisba Anguissola al servizio dei re di Spagna" was the basis.

For the artistic aspects of Sofonisba's Italian work, I followed Mina Gregori, "Fama e oblio di Sofonisba Anguissola," and various catalogue entries: for portraits, Rossana Sacchi; for religious works, Valerio Guazzoni; and for drawings, Giulio Bora and Bram de Klerck. Regarding Sofonisba's Spanish work and the portraits of the Spanish royal family which she painted in Italy after her return from Spain, I have quoted my own views from my essay "Sofonisba e il ritratto di rappresentanza uffiziale nella corte spagnola" and from the catalogue entries for the Spanish portraits, sometimes supplementing them.

Childhood and Youth in Cremona[1]

Sofonisba Anguissola was born under a lucky star. Her home, her native city, her era contributed to help her realize her talent, but, above all it was her strong personality that determined how and why she succeeded.

The exact date of her birth is unknown. After carefully weighing the circumstances and trying to reconcile her life dates, contemplating her works, especially the self-portraits, and tracing their evolution, the conclusion is that she must have been born around 1535, or perhaps slightly later.[2]

Cremona, her city of birth, was recovering around this time from outbreaks of the plague in 1511 and 1524, and from the chaos of the wars between the French and the Imperial Army, which had affected the city. The victory at Pavia in 1525 ensured the supremacy of Emperor Charles V in Italy. After the death of the last member of the Sforza family in 1535, the duchy of Milan, to which Cremona belonged, was assumed first by Charles V and afterward by his son Philip (later Philip II), who was invested by his father as Duke of Milan in 1540. A period of peace and prosperity then ensued. Cremona soon became one of the most important cities of the Po Basin. The government in Milan intervened little in the daily affairs of the cities and smaller communities, and the new authorities were not perceived as an occupational force. Everyone was grateful that they assured peace and civic order.

The textile trade became a particular source of wealth in Cremona. Half-wool cloth and flannels from Cremona were known and sought after throughout Europe. Soon the population of Cremona increased once more. At the time of Sofonisba's birth, about 20,000 inhabitants lived in the city, a significant number for that period.[3]

The arts blossomed. Construction projects began, which yielded work for painters and sculptors. Religious and secular music, a great tradition in Cremona nurtured from the 13th century onward, came to life again. Literature and poetry flourished. In the spirit of the Renaissance, the individual gained self-worth; personal initiative and talent found fertile soil here and elsewhere in Italy, wherever economic conditions permitted.

Self-confidence increased not only for men but also for women, and the latter, especially, were encouraged and supported by eminent patrons. When Baldassare Castiglione published *Il cortegiano* (The courtier) in 1528, he did not neglect the *cortegiana*, but rather demanded that she should develop her abilities just as the men did. Both the inner and the outer beauty of women, the beauty of body and mind, were challenged. The impact of the book, which was enormous, cannot be comprehended easily today. Women of cultivated society throughout Italy felt inspired. Granted, at first there were only a few, among them Vittoria Colonna and Isabella d'Este—women of high social standing such as Castiglione must have had in mind, whose potential and talents were significant enough to rise above the average. But the path was paved. Cities even competed by claiming to have the brightest, and yet most attractive, women within their walls.

The education of men and women was no longer a matter of chance but the result of careful planning. Families took pride not only in the accomplishments of their sons but also their daughters, who were well versed in all the arts. Within Cremona's immediate surroundings, in Mantua and Brescia, a number of highly literate ladies could be found. At the time of Sofonisba's birth, the scholar Marco Gerolamo Vida had taken on the education of a gifted young girl, Partenia Gallerati, in Cremona itself.[4]

Despite the new attitude toward the education of women, it is remarkable how quickly women of that generation filled their new role, considering the strong resistance still prevalent in less enlightened circles. A balancing act was necessary: women might be as capable and educated as the men, but could not flaunt their talents. Castiglione recognized the problem and recommended that women strive to maintain a difficult medium—*una mediocrità difficile;* the motto of women who dared venture into the men's domain was *discrezione*.

The scholar Vida and Sofonisba's father, Amilcare Anguissola, were friends. In their intellectual circle the topic of education, especially that of young girls, was a subject of discussion. Amilcare must have resolved to set theory into practice with his own children.[5]

He had married the still very young Bianca Ponzoni around 1533. Sofonisba's parents both came from the aristocracy of

PLATE • 5

Since the original from the collection of the Earl of Spencer in Althorp was not available for display, this slightly different, larger copy serves to help document Sofonisba's repeated pursuit of the theme at hand. The figures, of about the same size as in the original, are here surrounded by substantially more open space, which makes them appear further removed and lends the painting a somewhat odd character. This expansion was not added in retrospect, as has been suggested. In the original, both figures are fitted tightly into the picture plane and the spinet has been severely cropped, which makes the artist's intention of showing a scene taken directly from life successful. In the posthumous copy, however, the impetus changes to become the timeless admiration of an artist at the spinet.

According to early descriptions, the original was signed and dated, but over the course of time both inscription and date have faded. In 1766 *Sophonisba Anguisciola virgo se ipsum pinxit iussu Ami... patris...*, could be deciphered, but in 1872 evidently only *Sophonisba Anguisciola iussu patris.* Stylistically the work dates from Sofonisba's time in Cremona, even though British descriptions gave the date as 1561 or 1563.

The opinion of Caroli (1987, 130-31), that this self-portrait is not of Sofonisba but rather of her sister Lucia is not convincing. In the *Self-Portrait* from the Castello Sforzesco (Milan), as well as in Sofonisba's *The Chess Game* (plate 6), Lucia is shown with very different features–her face is narrower and the eyes are less bulging.

Compared to Sofonisba's earlier *Self-Portrait at the Spinet* (Naples, Museo di Capodimonte) this painting is actually a double portrait, even if the old maidservant, whom she had immortalized in the *The Chess Game,* remains in the background. The artist here looks more formal and official than in the Naples portrait, but she still sees herself in the context of her family, and there is no reference to her future career.

Exh. cat. Cremona 1994, no. 14 (A. Gilardi)

—SYLVIA FERINO-PAGDEN

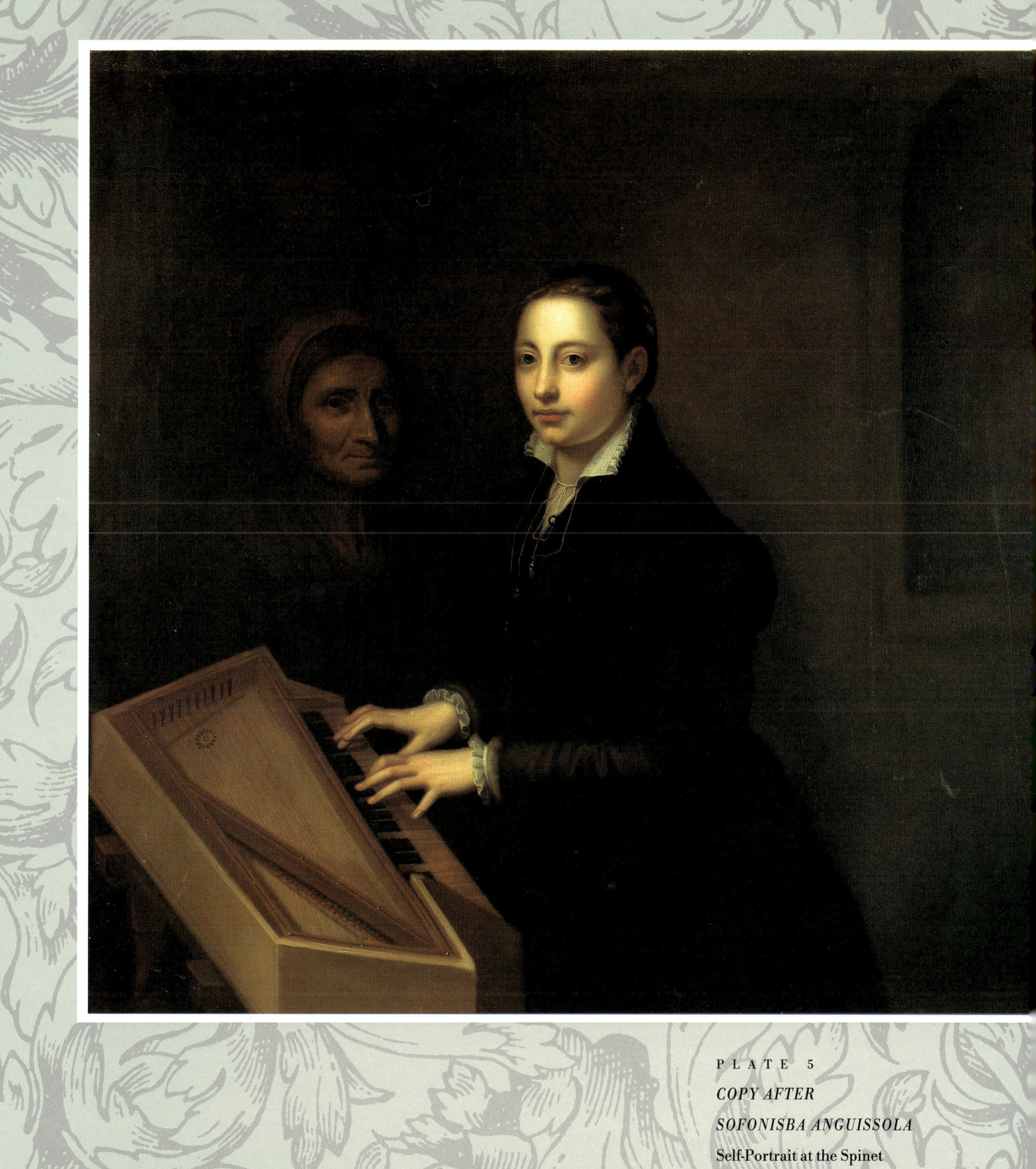

PLATE 5

COPY AFTER

SOFONISBA ANGUISSOLA

Self-Portrait at the Spinet

Oil on canvas, 42 1/2 x 42 1/8 in.

Goodwood, West Sussex,

Goodwood House

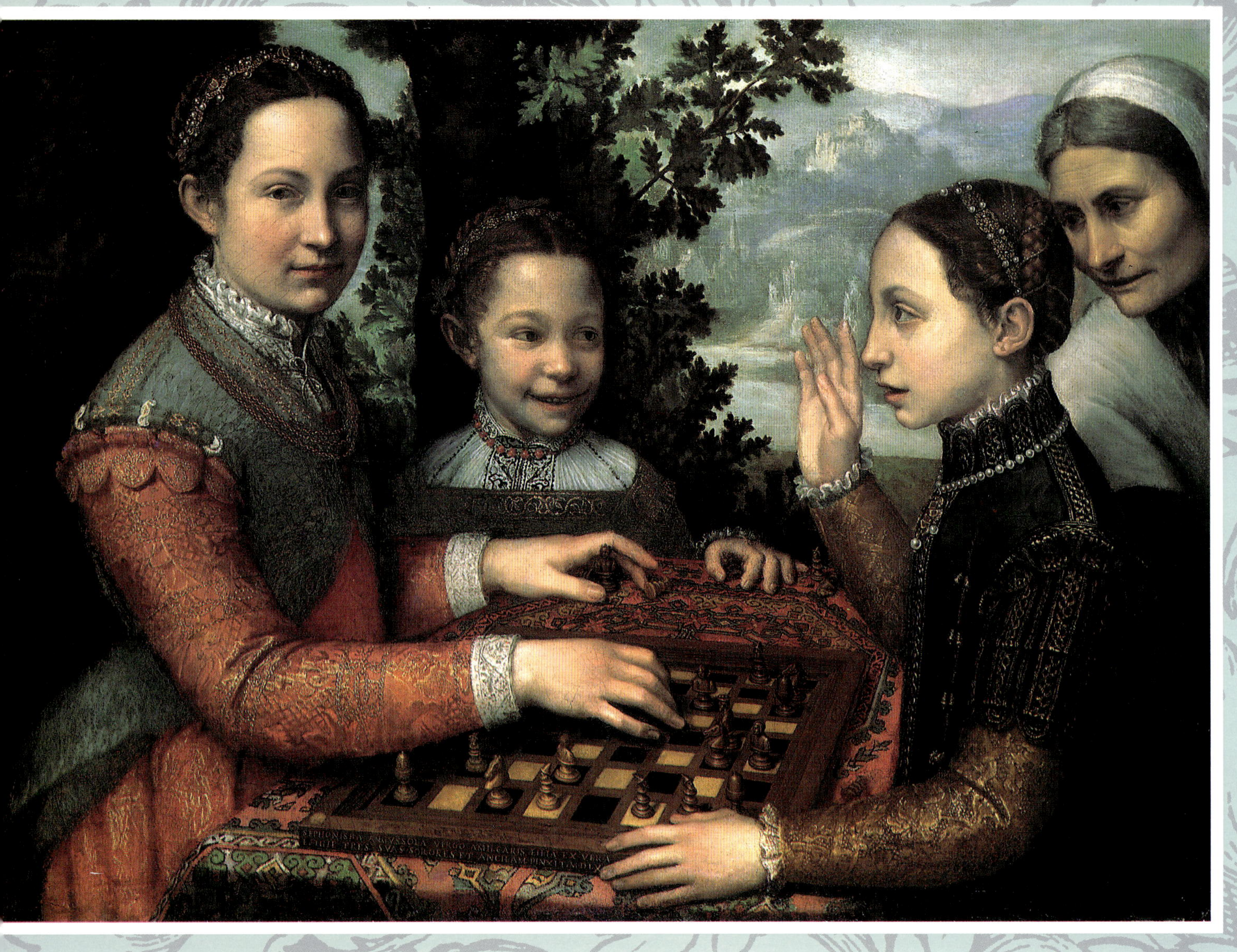

P L A T E 6

SOFONISBA ANGUISSOLA

The Chess Game

Oil on canvas, 28 3/8 x 38 1/8 in.

Inscribed on the chessboard:

SOPHONISBA ANGUSSOLA

VIRGO AMILCARIS FILIA EX

VERA EFFIGIE TRES SUAS

SORORES ET ANCILAM

PINXIT MDLV

Poznan, Muzeum Narodowe,

inv. no. MNP MO 39

P L A T E ◆ 6

This painting is considered Sofonisba's undisputed masterpiece. With its genre-like theme, its emotive rendering of the sisters playing chess in the presence of the maidservant and especially its unaffected, direct dialogue, it represented a completely new approach for all of Italian painting. Sofonisba's sisters are grouped around a chessboard, which rests on a small table covered with a Holbein rug. They are situated outdoors, with a view over the landscape in the distance to the right. The tallest of the sisters is Lucia, who is the third-born (and also became an excellent painter) looking outward from the picture on the left. Opposite Lucia, in clear profile, the rhetorically adroit and humanistically talented fourth-born, is Minerva. In the center is the fifth-born, Europa, who would also become a painter, seen here with an impish smile. New in this presentation is the combination of individual portrayals engaged in one collective activity, the chess game, while on the surface it appears as though the artist has only seized a moment from everyday life. The linking of the observation of nature with *storia,* action—the activity being a fictional one that takes place on the chess board—demonstrates the young artist's intellectual demands of her medium.

As the *Giocco d'ingenio e di arte,* chess was preferred to gambling games by Renaissance humanists such as Baldassare Castiglione and Marco Gerolamo Vida. According to tradition, it was also the game of the amazons or of maidens in general, as confirmed later by Torquato Tasso, since the queens in the game are allowed the greatest freedom of movement (Guazzoni in exh. cat. Cremona 1994, 68). In Sofonisba's painting, two maidens playing a game that is appropriate to their social status are engaged in a debate, on intellectual terrain in which they enjoy equality with men. The disagreement may be about the opposing black queen, gleefully held by Lucia in her left hand, which she has just taken but which perhaps, as in a play written by Marco Gerolamo Vida, *Scacchia ludus,* in the end will be victorious over the white king.

The painting was described by Vasari in 1566 as being in the possession of the Anguissola family, but it later entered the collection of Fulvio Orsinis in Rome. It was owned in 1600 by the Farnese and purchased in the 19th century by Luciano Bonaparte. In 1823 it belonged to Count Athanasius Raczynski in Paris and later to the museum in Poznan.

Exh. cat. Cremona 1994, no. 3 (R. Sacchi)

—SYLVIA FERINO-PAGDEN

the city. The Cremonese branch of the Anguissola family was less influential and prosperous than their powerful relatives in Piacenza. Bianca's family, however, was one of the most prominent in Cremona.[6]

Amilcare, who was born out of wedlock but acknowledged as the legitimate son of Annibale, owned very little property in the city or the countryside. He supported his family through the most diverse business enterprises, from trading books and medicine or aromatic herbs (a business in which his father had been engaged) to purchasing grain for the city administration. A highly regarded patrician, he belonged to the city council of ten, representing the interests of Cremona not only in business but also on diplomatic missions to the central government in Milan. In Cremona Amilcare also looked after the poor and adjudicated civic problems.

The young couple moved into the Anguissola family home opposite San Giorgio, in which Amilcare's father (Annibale) and his grandfather (Lazzaro) had resided before him. The house exists to this day, in what is now the Via Pellegrino Tibaldi. It is one of the massive, spacious, palazzo-like houses in the city that are built around a small garden.

Here six daughters and one son were born: Sofonisba, Elena, Lucia, Minerva and Europa; then, finally, the son, Asdrubale, followed by another daughter, Anna Maria. The names of the children tell much about the parental home. Sofonisba's and Asdrubale's names were chosen in keeping with the family's traditional affinity for the Carthaginian dynasty. This preference of the Lombard family for Rome's major opponents must have sprung from the sense of historic independence that prevailed in the Italian alpine region. Hannibal had once "freed" Cisalpine Gaul and the Roman colonies Cremona, Placentia and Mutina. Elena and Lucia had their grandmothers' names, choices which satisfied family requirements and their parents' personal preferences. The names of Minerva and Europa represented the humanist tradition. Only the name of the last-born remains without recognizable references, unless one would like to link the name to the two great women in Christianity.[7]

The children seem to have been born in close succession, within about three years each. An exact date of birth is known only for Asdrubale: 1551. There must have been a greater span of years between his birth and that of the last child, Anna Maria, than was the case with the previous children.[8]

Amilcare was much more successful in educating his children than in tending to his business. With the increasing number of offspring, practical concerns intensified his desire to educate them. A good education would raise the girls' esteem in the community and would eventually lower the dowry required by prospective suitors.[9]

His first, most successful educational "object" was Sofonisba. The name he gave his firstborn, that of Hannibal's niece, was more than mere homage to the Carthaginians. Boccaccio described Sofonisba, the Carthaginian queen, in *De claris mulieribus* as a very brave woman and other authors praised her as "di bellezza eccellentissima, e nelle lettere, e nella musica esertatissima"–virtues and abilities that matched the feminine ideal of the day and Amilcare's as well.

Painting, however, was not among the activities considered suitable for women, although Castiglione had listed it as one of the arts women should practice. It was too closely related to craftsmanship and associated with too much physical exertion (in fresco painting, for example) to be considered appropriate for a lady. The existence of earlier women painters was largely ignored—Marcia, a painter from antiquity, was too far removed in time; more contemporary examples were from a different sphere, the convent. The painting of miniatures in convents was viewed more as a craft for women than as an art. In the Netherlands the issue was treated very differently. There, women and girls from families of painters automatically participated in the family occupation.

The zeitgeist dictated the fact that Amilcare Anguissola and Bianca Ponzoni decided to educate their many daughters in accord with the new fashion. The decision to let the eldest apprentice with a painter, however, was almost revolutionary. According to sources of the time, it seems to have raised eyebrows not only in Cremona but other cities as well.[10] Sofonisba's mother, Bianca, undoubtedly participated in making the decision. She was not only a very beautiful woman but also a strong personality whose opinions mattered to her husband—too much, as the scholar Vida told Amilcare in a long letter, despite his appreciation of talented women.[11] In the eyes of the scholar, Bianca must have occasionally crossed the boundaries of *misura*. She was as much an influence on her household as her husband. Sofonisba, Lucia and Europa memorialized her in superb paintings. Sofonisba painted her in a festive gown (Berlin, Staatliche Museen Preussischer Kulturbesitz), and Lucia a few years later in everyday attire (Rome, Galleria Borghese). Europa's painting of her mother was sent to Sofonisba in Madrid—unfortunately, its whereabouts is no longer known—and the entire court evidently admired it.[12]

In 1546 Sofonisba and her sister Elena, who was approximately one year younger, were apprenticed to Bernardino Campi. They were both about ten, the age at which boys began an apprenticeship. This information is passed down by Alessandro Lamo, a learned Cremonese contemporary of Sofonisba. One reason for the affiliation with Bernardino was probably Amilcare's supervision of the construction and interior decoration of San Sigismondo. Bernardino Campi was an important contributor to that project. In 1585 Lamo writes in his treatise on art:

In this year 1546, Bernardino Campi instructed the sisters Sofonisba and Elena Anguissola in the art of drawing. . . . When both made good progress and both wished to pursue the instruction in art more deeply, and the father wished to oblige this noble pursuit, he found accommodations for them at the house of Bernardino, with the intention that the nobility and worth of his two children should make the profession of the painter noble and respected in this city. Bernardino, who introduced them to art with patience and a gentle manner, who critiqued without causing fear and praised without spoiling, grew so dear to them that they spent three years in his house, where they felt as happy surrounded by the kindness of Bernardino's wife as they did about the excellent instruction in art that they received.[13]

Evidently the drawing lessons by Bernardino Campi, which at first had taken place in the parental home, were expanded to become regular instruction at the artist's house. His studio was there and so were all the necessary materials. The caring attention by the painter's wife, so emphasized by Lamo, must mean that the girls were taken into the private quarters, away from the male, rougher world of the studio, and placed in the charge of the lady of the house, which also protected their reputation. According to a letter to her former teacher, later written by Sofonisba from Spain, the painter's parents and sister also received them with the utmost warmth. This twice-documented kind reception by the family of the painter shows how much the whole household was aware of the unusual situation, and what excitement and inconvenience ensued from having two such refined young ladies in the house. The social differences between the families make it unlikely that the two girls lived with the painter's family full-time. After painting practice, they must have received their other lessons at home, and surely spent their nights in the safety of their parents' house.[14]

Lamo's comments explain how and why Amilcare arrived at the idea to apprentice his daughters to a painter. At least in part, the girls themselves wished to go. Previous instruction in drawing must have taken place, motivated by an early awareness of their special talents. Their father cultivated them as he fostered the musical and literary development of his other daughters. In addition, Amilcare wanted to set an example. By letting his own children learn through a regular apprenticeship to a painter, he wanted to inspire members of other distinguished families to include such studies in their children's education. He wanted to "ennoble" such instruction and make it acceptable by the example of his own children. In particular, he must have had young ladies in mind.[15]

The instruction by Bernardino Campi, an elegant mannerist who produced smooth paintings, must have been the foundation for Sofonisba's preference for pleasant, gentle, religious scenes. Mainly, however, she was influenced by Bernardino's grand and famous portraiture, of which only a few examples have survived. Bernardino taught her the fundamentals of drawing. We know from his own account how he approached teaching. In his *Parere sopra la pittura* he says: "First one must learn to copy any kind of drawing, selecting only the very best." We also know from Lamo about the examples Bernardino used. Lamo relates that the artist spared no expense to buy drawings by the brilliant Camillo Boccaccino, whose great art played such an important role in Cremona.[16] From the beginning both sisters must also have been instructed in the art of portraiture *dal naturale*, a subject that was not only one of the master's strengths but probably considered most suitable for young ladies.

They learned what was practical: portraits in relatively small format could easily be painted at home. Amilcare here adhered to traditional thinking, which dictated that his daughters should learn to paint like professionals but work at home. Their gender and social position ruled out any possibility that they might engage in their profession in the company of male craftsmen in a studio, or even work on public building commissions. It is perhaps because of this early specialization, which caused the neglect of *invenzione*, the "creation" of sacred or profane multi-figured scenes, that Sofonisba remained a copyist of religious scenes all her life and never painted profane ones.[17]

After Bernardino Campi moved to Milan in 1549, the sisters' instruction continued under Bernardino Gatti, whose influence was equally profound for Sofonisba. Her instruction in true painterly expression seems to be his doing. His execution, his handling of color, his Correggesque softness and Leonardesque character of facial features is evident in Sofonisba's works.[18]

The quality of the first extant painting by the young Sofonisba, her *The Artist's Sister in the Garb of a Nun*, 1551 (plate 1) must be appreciated in light of her outstanding schooling by these two masters. Elena's face, with its shy yet open expression, is touching. The figure is a sensual pleasure, with the white woolen tunic, the fluid drapery and the finely tuned brown shadows on the cuffs of the sleeves, enlivened by the brick-red prayer book and the evenly dark green background. The artist's two most prominent characteristics are already apparent: her interest in capturing her subject's personality and her delight in the aesthetic and beautiful.

Other earlier works must have existed but are now lost. Gerolamo Vida, her father's scholar-friend, who must have followed Amilcare's educational experiment with interest, lists the young artist in a document of 1550 under the heading "inter egregios pictores nostri temporis."[19] Even if his praise may have been somewhat emphatic to please his friend, it must have been based on existing works.

The painting of her sister as a nun signals a change in the Anguissola household. Elena left her parents' home and Cremona to enter the Dominican abbey of San Vincenzo in Mantua, pursuing one of the traditional life choices of an educated woman at the time. It can be assumed that she continued to paint there, although no works are known to exist or are described anywhere.[20] With the portrait of her sister, Sofonisba proves that she has developed her own artistic style; the actual apprenticeship is thereby concluded.

After their separation from Elena the remaining sisters seem to have become closer. Sofonisba ended her studio education and passed her knowledge on to her sisters, as a number of copies of her own paintings by less experienced hands seem to indicate. Sofonisba devoted herself in particular to Lucia, who died early. Lucia had a talent for music and a special penchant for painting, demonstrated by the very few paintings by her that exist.[21] Minerva, a gifted woman of letters, is thought to have painted as well, and also must have been taught by the older sister.[22]

Sofonisba herself continued painting with various inspirations and goals. Two kinds of works soon brought her fame: her humorous genre-like scenes and her portraits, which most often depicted members of her family. The youth, charm

At least three versions are known of this first full-length portrait by Sofonisba, of which the one in Baltimore (acquired in 1927) today is considered the undisputed original (after de Tolnay in 1941, 155, assumed collaboration by Lucia Anguissola). A similarity with Giovanni Battista Moroni is obvious. Compare, for example, Moroni's *Michel de l'Hospital* in Milan (Pinacoteca Ambrosiana). Not without reason had the portrait been attributed to Moroni himself, until Bernard Berenson (1907, 163) declared first the example from a private collection and later the portrait in Baltimore to be by Sofonisba Anguissola. The identification of the subject was only made in 1986, when the canvas was relined and the inscription on the verso was detected. The full inscription is *Max(imilianus) Sta(mpa) Mar(chio) Son(cini) III-aet(atis) an(norum) VIIII* (Simons 1986, 117). Massimiliano Stampa was the only son of Ermes, second marchese of Soncino, who died in 1557. This explains the reason for the "official" portrait of this third marchese, the nine-year-old Massimiliano, who, although still a child, is equipped with all the attributes of his position—a black suit, a dagger, gloves and a ring. The column on which the boy leans on is also a symbol for power. The depiction of space in this version shows some uncertainty of perspective, a point that was improved in the later version now in a private collection. The dignified grandeur of the young marchese contrasts with the still childlike fragility of his slightly drooping shoulders. The concentrated quiver in the face of this child who has had to grow up too quickly after the loss of the father is masterfully realized from a psychological point of view.

The motif of the sleeping dog is taken from Albrecht Dürer's *Melancholia,* but also evidently based on a study from nature (de Tolnay 1941).

The Stampa were a powerful aristocratic family in 16th-century Lombardy. Ermes Stampa had commissioned Bernardino Campi, Sofonisba's teacher, to paint altarpieces for his family estate, Soncino, which accounts for the connection with Sofonisba.

Exh. cat. Cremona 1994, no. 11 (R. Sacchi)

—*ALEXANDER WIED*

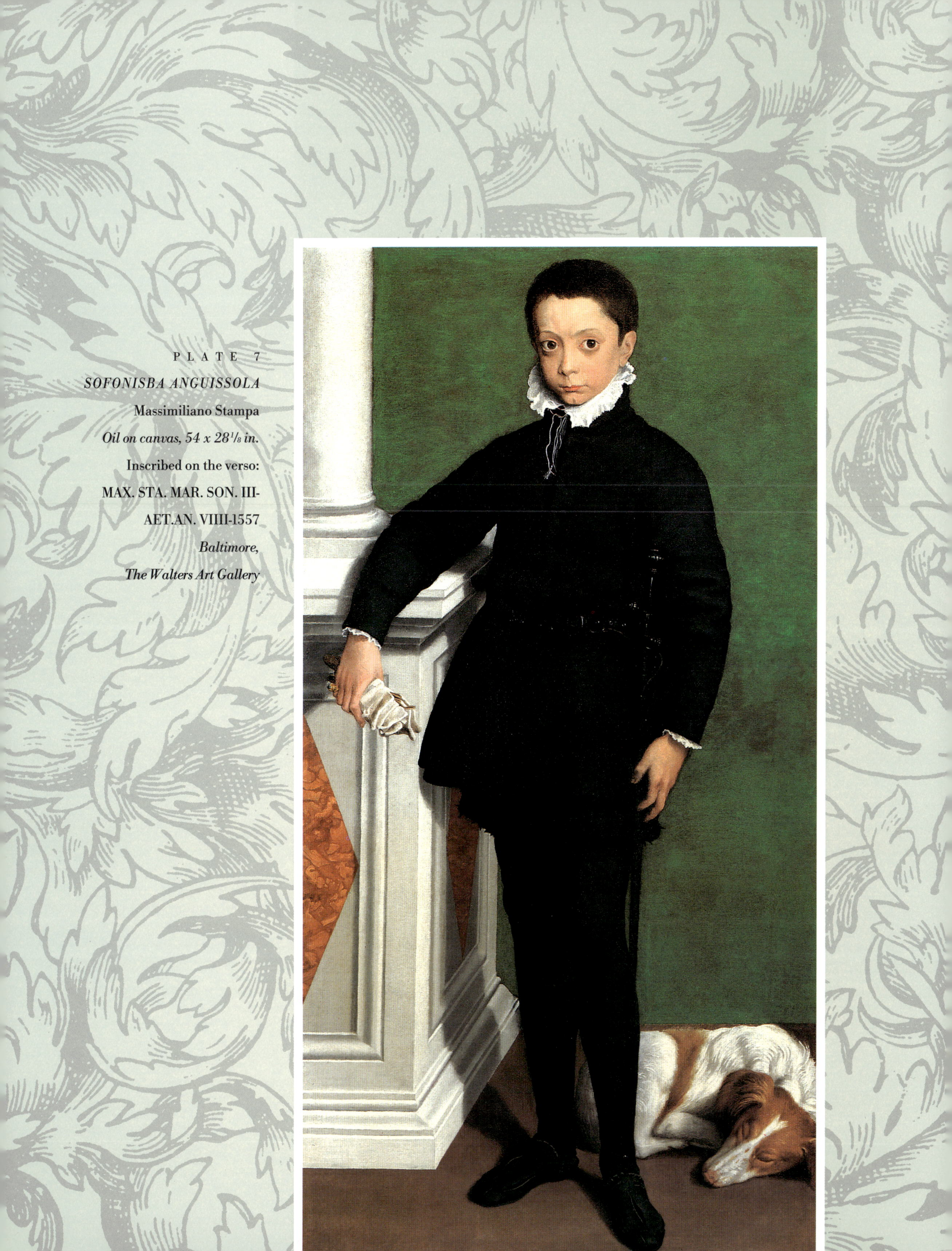

PLATE 7

SOFONISBA ANGUISSOLA

Massimiliano Stampa

Oil on canvas, 54 x 28 1/8 in.

Inscribed on the verso:

MAX. STA. MAR. SON. III-

AET.AN. VIIII-1557

Baltimore,

The Walters Art Gallery

P L A T E • 8

This impressive portrait, dated 1556, reveals Sofonisba's already developed ability to depict her subjects with psychological insight. The dignified earnestness of the monk is mixed with the cheerful composure of a man who has peace of mind and a firm belief in his faith. He is still young, but seems mature. His skin has a healthy glow, the eyes are gray, the beard is dark brown and the hair on his head is beginning to thin. The slight turn of the head and the asymmetrical diagonal of the cape give the picture a liveliness that is reminiscent of Lorenzo Lotto's portraiture (Caroli assumes a direct influence by Lotto).

The subject is most likely the monk Ippolito Chizzola. This identification, already suggested by F. Odorici (1853, 194) is based on a notice collected by Ottavio Rossi in his *Elogi historici di Bresciani illustri* (1620, 350), in which a portrait of Chizzola by Sofonisba from Cremona is mentioned. In addition, the monk wears the habit of the Laterans, an order to which Chizzola, in fact, belonged.

The inscription is assumed to be original, but the "i" in Anguissola, which is uncommon for Sofonisba's Cremonese works, is a later addition.

Exh. cat. Cremona 1994, no. 4 (R. Sacchi)

—*ALEXANDER WIED*

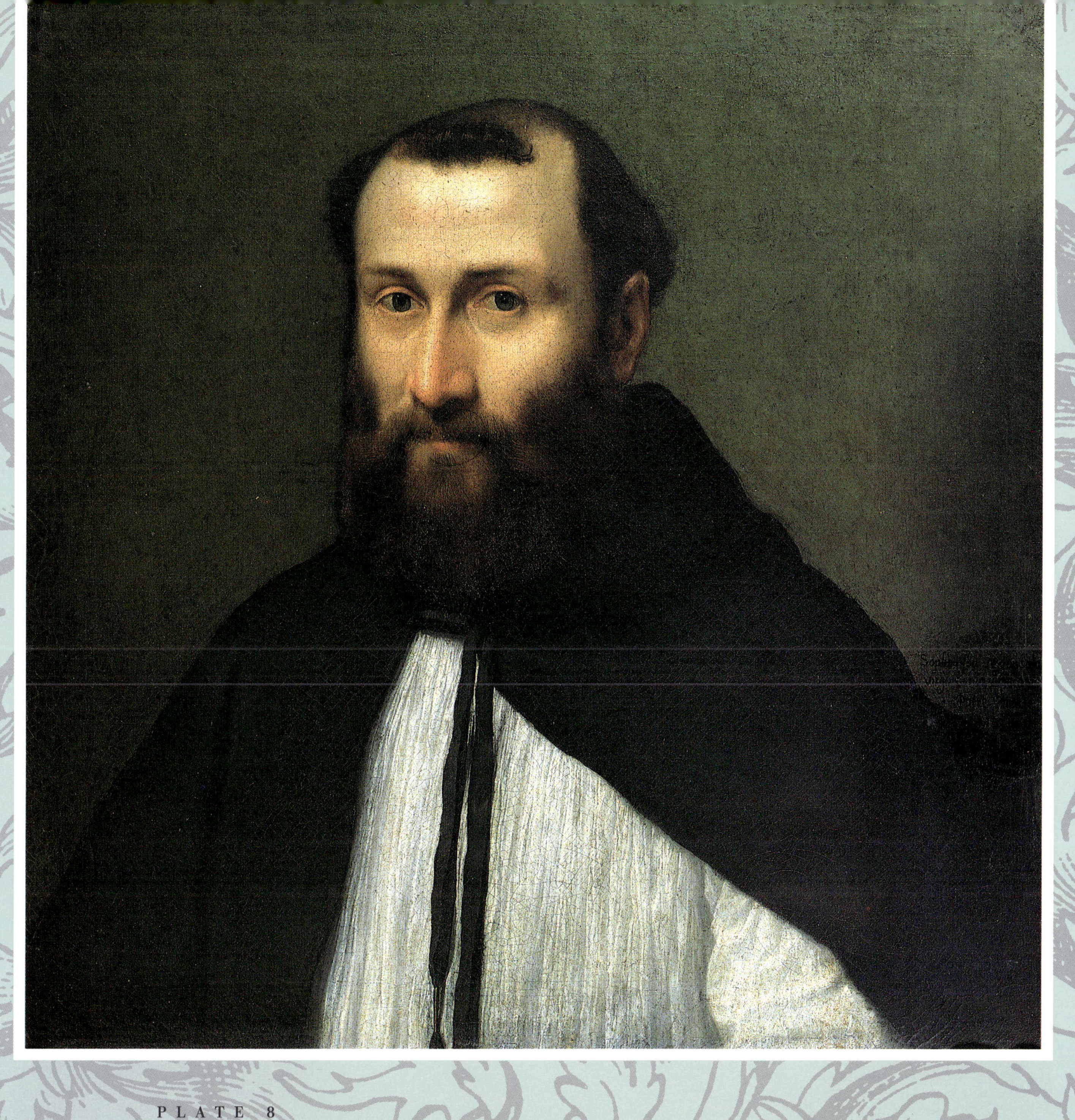

PLATE 8

SOFONISBA ANGUISSOLA

Portrait of a Monk

Oil on canvas, 22 ½ x 20 ⅞ in.

Inscribed at the right side:

Sophonisba Anguissola/Virgo

Coram Amilcare/Patre (m)

Pinxit/MDLVI

Brescia, Pinacoteca Tosio

Martinengo

and pleasing femininity of the young artist surely contributed to the admiration of her talent.

Of the genre-like scenes two drawings remain, executed directly after the portrait of her sister Elena. One is *A Laughing Girl Teaching an Older Woman to Read*, an activity the girl finds very amusing (Florence, Galleria degli Uffizi; variation on a scene by Jacob Bos, Amsterdam, Rijksmuseum). Judging by the facial features, it represents one of Sofonisba's sisters, probably Lucia, because of her age and the similarity of the slanted eyes with later renderings.[23] The drawing so stunned contemporaries with its naturalness and originality that it was shown to Michelangelo, who was evidently much taken with the artist. Tommaso Cavalieri, Michelangelo's friend, recounts that the master, after contemplating the scene, gave Sofonisba a further, more difficult assignment: to draw a crying boy. Sofonisba met the challenge with ease. She sent the master a drawing of *Boy Bitten by a Crab* (Naples, Museo di Capodimonte), her brother, Asdrubale. One sister, who is not rushing to his aid, watches the dilemma with a smile. Judging by her age, she could be Minerva, who was an avid reader and may have contributed the fable from which the scene was taken.[24]

Tommaso Cavalieri[25] emphasizes that the drawings were not only beautiful but also truly inventive creations, *invenzione*. He thereby awarded the young Sofonisba the highest praise for an independent artist of the time. Sofonisba drew or painted several more of these humorous scenes, of which Giorgio Vasari, who was one of her first biographers,[26] said admiringly, "non si può veder cosa più graziosa, né più simile alvero." The painter Francesco Salviati praised several drawings that circulated in Rome.[27]

Sofonisba's portraits soon became collector's items. Her first extant *Self-Portrait* (plate 2) dates from 1554. Bust-length, it shows her holding a small book with the careful inscription "Sophonisba Anguissola virgo seipsam fecit 1554." Many of her early works are similarly inscribed; unfortunately, however, they are not dated. The inscriptions make it possible to determine her early style reliably, upon which her later work is based. The painting indicates how young the artist still was, although already well known, and that success had not spoiled her. She depicts herself in a simple dark dress, brightened by a ruffled collar which is brushed on with fluffy dots. Her hair is pulled back austerely and held with a plain net. Her large, observant eyes indicate that she looks at the world and at herself very closely.

Many other self-portraits from every phase of her life follow this one. Several are evidently influenced by the works of Caterina van Hemessen, for example her *Self-Portrait at the Spinet* (Naples, Museo di Capodimonte) and *Self Portrait at the Easel* (plate 4). It is not known whether she was familiar with the work of the Flemish artist directly or through prints, or whether she had only heard of it.

More than a dozen self-portraits are still extant,[28] making Sofonisba one of the artists with the largest number of self-portraits.

What was her motive for producing them? Her presentation of herself rules out vanity. In her early years in Cremona she must have used her own image to experiment and practice her art. When her paintings became successful, her father used them to promote her work. Later in life, when she was far away from home, the paintings assumed the role of photographs, used by the artist to document how she is feeling and let her family see her appearance.

In addition to her self-portraits, she painted more ambitious portraits of her family: a humorous *Chess Game* and *The Family Group* (Nivaa, Nivaagaards Malerisamling), paintings whose animation and coloring indicate the range of the artist's potential. The two group portraits which helped to spread Sofonisba's fame were among the works Vasari admired when he visited the family in Cremona,

The Chess Game (plate 6) shows again how Sofonisba is able to turn an allegorical scene of Netherlandish origin—here the *Chess Players* by Lucas van Leyden, which she knew through a work by Giulio Campi[29]—into a view of everyday life. With her rendition of domestic life she prefigures all the elements of true genre painting.[30]

A few years later, around 1557, Sofonisba painted the impressive *Family Group*, as we know from Vasari. An equally beautiful portrait of *Amilcare in His Old Age*, probably painted by Europa, is still in Cremona (Cremona, Museo Civico), which rounds out the impression one derives of this distinguished man from the group portrait.[31] Sofonisba's group portraits and the portrait of her mother (Berlin, Staatliche Museen Preussischer Kulturbesitz) give the viewer a lively idea of not just the cheerful art of her youth but also the life of the artist and her family. Portraits of friends of the family or other personalities include, for example, the *Portrait of a Monk* (plate 8), a *Dominican Astrologer* (formerly Terzo d'Aquileia, Collection Calligaris) and an *Old Man with a Toga* (Stamford, Burghley House Collection).

Sofonisba's apprenticeship and first big successes were followed by a period in which Amilcare tried to broaden his daughter's mind as well as help her reputation spread outside of Cremona. The family's economic situation had taken a turn for the worse and the number of their children had grown. The moment had come for him to realize material gain from his daughter's abilities in a manner that would be compatible with her social position.

The year 1556 was a period for travel. In March, Amilcare had tried to establish contact with Ercole d'Este, duke of Ferrara, by sending one of Sofonisba's self-portraits to the court—probably the *Self-Portrait* of 1554 that is now in Vienna (plate 2).[32] In February of the same year Sofonisba was received very favorably at the court of Mantua, where she had visited to see her sister Elena. Amilcare may have planned that she continue her tour from there to Ferrara. In a letter to the duchess of Mantua, Amilcare thanks her for the kindness shown his daughters.[33] Sofonisba must have given the duchess a work as a present, perhaps one of the paintings that later appeared in the Gonzaga catalogue,[34] and was rewarded with a gift. This visit proved to be important for her artistic development. She viewed the art

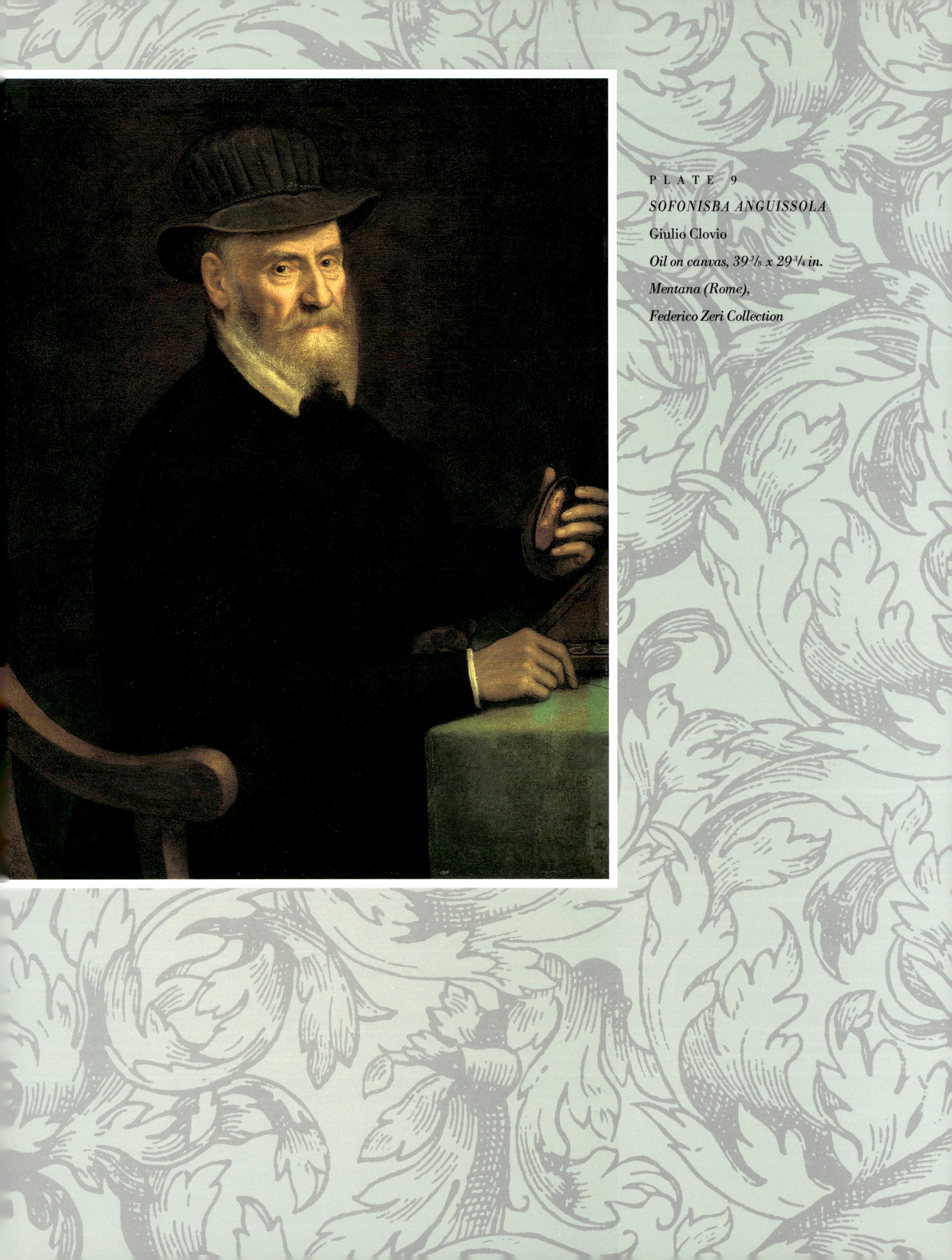

PLATE 9

SOFONISBA ANGUISSOLA

Giulio Clovio

Oil on canvas, 39 3/8 x 29 3/4 in.

Mentana (Rome),

Federico Zeri Collection

P L A T E ◆ 9

This portrait, which is large compared to the format generally used by Sofonisba in Cremona, was still thought in the 19th century to be by Titian (Sambo 1985, 175). At that time it was part of the collection of Charles Townley; only in the Berenson edition of 1968 (vol. 1, 14; vol. 3, ill. 1970) is it attributed to Sofonisba Anguissola. The identity of the subject is confirmed by a comparison with Clovio's portrait by El Greco (Museo di Capodimonte, Naples; color ill. in Giononi-Visani–Gamulin 1993, 83).

The portrait shows Clovio, the most famous miniaturist of his time, in a domestic environment, sitting at a table and looking directly at the viewer. Only the hat lends the picture a respectful, formal character. Before him he has a box with paints, and in his left hand he holds a miniature portrait, which may depict Levina Teerlinc, a Flemish miniature painter who had completed her apprenticeship with Clovio in the 1540s.

Unfortunately, no information is given anywhere about direct contact between Clovio and Sofonisba, but the inventory of Clovio's estate records one of Sofonisba's works (which is no longer identifiable), and Sofonisba's fame makes it probable that the two met occasionally in 1556, the time of the portrait. In that year Clovio visited the Farnese family in Parma and Piacenza, towns in which the Anguissola had numerous contacts.

Exh. cat. Cremona 1994, no. 5 (R. Sacchi)

—ALEXANDER WIED

PLATE • 10

Painted on a finished, round piece of wood that may have been the lid of a box, this portrait was part of the copious collection of miniatures belonging to Cardinal Leopoldo de' Medici. If identical with an image cited in the inventory of 1655, a "roundel with head and half-torso of a woman, with gold frame, made of lathed walnut," it probably stems from the property of the Rovere family in Urbino, with whom Sofonisba kept in touch after her departure for Spain. In the inventories of the Uffizi it has been considered a self-portrait of Sofonisba since 1890 (Meloni Trkulja 1976, 38-39), and has recently again been included among the artist's oeuvre by Maria Kusche. Since Sofonisba is representing herself here as a lady of rank and not just as an artist, it must be dated around 1559, the time of her appointment as lady-in-waiting to Isabel of Valois, or perhaps the first year of her residence in Spain.

In this small portrait the artist seems very concerned with her appearance. She depicts herself with earrings, a necklace and a painstakingly reproduced hairstyle, with delicately painted curls around the forehead and jewelry braided into her hair, signaling a new stage of artistic self-appraisal or a new phase in her life in general, according to Kusche.

The same is true for another painting (Milan, private collection), in which Sofonisba portrayed herself in three-quarter size, in a magnificent, jewel-embroidered dress, wearing exquisite jewelry (Kusche in exh. cat. Cremona 1994, 138). Here, however, the viewer is puzzled by her utterly changed features. Compared to the rounded face with the wide cheeks and prominent cheekbones, here the graceful, heart-shaped face converges in a pointed chin (which is more typical of Minerva), and the large, dark eyes seem to justify the question of whether the model was not perhaps an entirely different person.

These works in the smallest of sizes were especially well suited as presents. They were easily transported and, with their intricate execution, particularly valued as precious objects for personal use.

Exh. cat. Cremona 1994, no. 17 (R. Sacchi)

—*SYLVIA FERINO-PAGDEN*

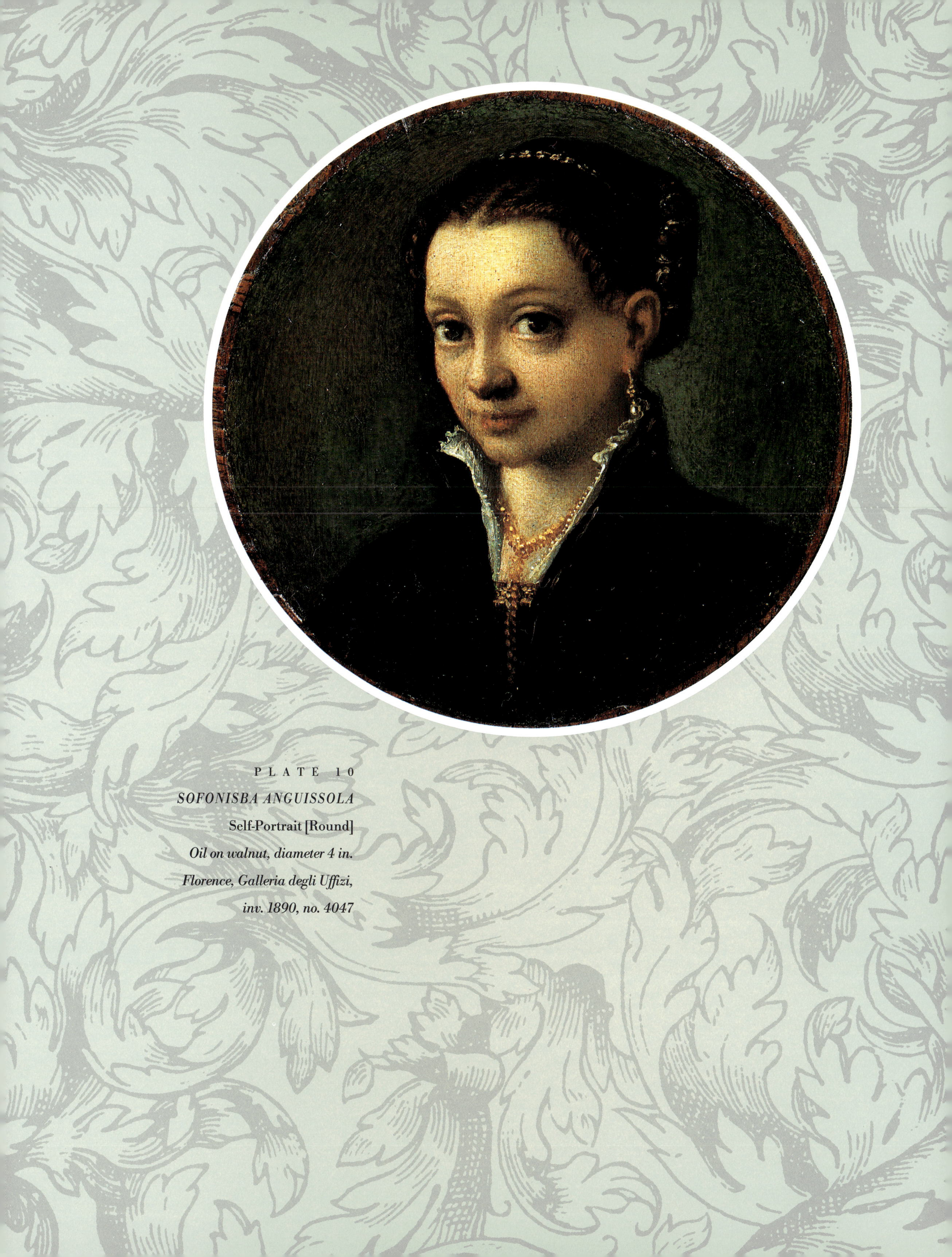

PLATE 10

SOFONISBA ANGUISSOLA

Self-Portrait [Round]

Oil on walnut, diameter 4 in.

Florence, Galleria degli Uffizi,

inv. 1890, no. 4047

of Giulio Romano and his followers, but, more important for her, Titian's representational court paintings.

Shortly thereafter she must have traveled to Parma, as indicated by *Giulio Clovio* (plate 9),[35] the famous miniaturist who lived there in 1556. Sofonisba painted him at work on a miniature of his student Levina Teerlinc. The objective of the journey must have been to receive an introduction to the art of this famous master of the miniature, while he was staying in the nearby city. This must have been done in conjunction with an introduction to the court at Parma by Margaret of Parma, daughter of Emperor Charles V, widow of Ottavio Farnese and subsequently governor of the Netherlands. Sofonisba's later contact with the Farnese must date to this encounter.

The first results of Clovio's advice were not long in coming. That same year (1556), the *Self-Portrait [in Miniature]* (plate 3) must have been painted, along with the *Self-Portrait* in Paris (Fondation Custodia, Institut Néerlandais),[36] which so closely reproduces the same facial features and which is signed 1556. The meeting with Clovio would be important in Sofonisba's later career. As an older woman, while living in Palermo and Genoa, she resumed miniature painting.

The stay in Parma was followed in 1559 by an episode which testifies to the demand for Sofonisba's self-portraits. Annibale Caro, the learned secretary of the duke of Parma, ardently wanted a self-portrait of Sofonisba, whose work he much admired. Amilcare, however, first delayed in fulfilling the request and finally sent the long-promised portrait to the duke, a gesture which the scholar registered with indignation.[37]

Sofonisba's larger paintings also reflect the artistic experiences of the year. In 1557 she painted *Bianca Ponzoni Anguissola* and the full-length *Massimiliano Stampa*, third Marchese of Soncino (plate 7). For the first one, she borrows the model's pose from Titian's portrayal of sitting ladies,[38] and a suggestion of Francesco Mazzola Parmigianino[39] is visible in the treatment of the fabric. In the portrait of the young Marchese of Soncino, her first depiction of a standing model, various influences are apparent: paintings by Alessandro Bonvicino Moretto and Giovanni Battista Moroni, which she must have known, and Titian's painting of the duke of Mantua.

Amilcare probably made a further attempt to promote his daughter in Urbino. Another self-portrait must have been sent there, probably identical to the small canvas *Self-Portrait [Round]* in Florence (plate 10).[40] This supposition is supported by the extraordinary interest the envoy of the duke of Urbino in Spain took in Sofonisba's life, repeatedly mentioning her in reports to his employer. It is not known whether Sofonisba ever visited Urbino. Soon there was interest in her in Florence as well, as indicated by the shipment of the drawing of her crying little brother by Tommaso Cavalieri in 1562.[41]

Meanwhile Amilcare, always maneuvering between his financial difficulties, his love of art and his wish to promote his daughter, reestablished contact with Michelangelo, which had been initiated over the young Sofonisba's drawings. In a letter of May 1557, Amilcare assures the revered painter that the tender affection bestowed by Michelangelo on the daughter means more to him than all the wealth in the world, and begs him to continue to help Sofonisba with advice: "I assure you that, if Sofonisba may count on your honored attention, her soaring spirit will so improve her studies that I expect the greatest successes." Amilcare does not hesitate to ask Michelangelo for his own drawings, which his daughter will return "colored in oils." This wish evidently materialized; a year later Amilcare writes a letter of deep gratitude for the interest shown in Sofonisba's painting: "that such an excellent nobleman, who exceeds all others with his talents, indeed condescends to praise and judge the painting of my daughter Sofonisba." He concludes by expressing the hope of meeting the master in person, adding that such a meeting will be in paradise, since for many reasons it is often not possible on earth to meet in body but only in spirit, as Michelangelo is always included in his and his family's thoughts.[42] Michelangelo's drawings may have helped Sofonisba's technique, but they had no more influence on furthering her creativity than the instruction of her Cremonese teachers had been able to achieve.

Two scenes are left from the remaining time in Cremona, a *Madonna Nursing the Child* (Italy, private collection) and *Holy Family* (plate 21). Both follow their models very closely, although Sofonisba imprints her own expression and soft technique. The first image is the Lombard interpretation of a Netherlandish original. The other is based on a drawing by Boccaccino, whose drawings, as we know, had been used as teaching material by Bernardino Campi.[43] The choice of these two examples reflects Sofonisba's preference for domestic scenes. She would never have attempted a tough religious theme, such as a crucifixion or a suffering saint, instead preferring pleasing devotional motifs and scenes from the life of the Christ Child. Her paintings were always intended for private use, never for a church or religious institution.

These sporadic contacts with various courts did not generate a permanent position for Sofonisba nor enable her to contribute to her family's financial resources. Life in Cremona followed a set routine. In the morning there was church service with the sisters, followed by work in the studio at home, teaching the sisters and supervising their exercises; in the afternoon, practicing the spinet, reading the classics or modern poets and an occasional visit here and there. Every so often there was a festivity or some other domestic activities. This must have been more or less her life, as we conclude from other contemporary sources.[44] The occasional trip to nearby courts and the first glimpses of wealth and of life without material worries, therefore, must have provided a very welcome diversion.

The future loomed dark. The gifts that resulted from these expensive, laborious travels must have relieved the financial burdens of the family only intermittently. Sofonisba supposedly received an offer of marriage in those years that had to be turned down because there was no dowry for her.[45] The lack of a dowry was indeed a problem of the greatest magnitude. Marriage was a family affair and the iron rule, at least in the patrician circles, was that the bride had to contribute to the upkeep of the new household.[46] The Anguissola family would encounter the problem caused by the lack of dowries for their daughters repeatedly. Was a marriage for Sofonisba really prevented only by the missing dowry? One must remember that the immense investment Amilcare had made in the education of this daughter, financially as well as intellectually, had not yet been amortized. It is entirely possible, therefore, that Amilcare may have prevented this marriage. Sofonisba herself does not seem to have suffered a broken heart, as shown by her cheerful acceptance of the new circumstances about to develop.

The Journey to Spain and Preparations in Milan[47]

Sooner than expected and entirely unanticipated in this guise, Sofonisba's life and that of her family were about to take a turn. From this point on she would be under the permanent patronage of a great ruler: Philip II of Spain, the most important sovereign for Italy and other parts of Europe.

The events that precede this change indicate the impact it had on Sofonisba and her family. The peace treaty ending the permanent state of war between France and Spain was signed on 3 April 1559 in Cateau-Cambrésis. News of this "blessed peace" was proclaimed in Cremona on 20 April and, according to Antonio Campi, was received with such *gaudio universale* that higher enthusiasm was unimaginable. Peace was of the greatest significance for northern Italy, where the devastating war years were still fresh in everyone's mind. The pledge for peace was convincing:

With this peace treaty it is decreed . . . that the catholic King Philip agrees to take Isabel, the eldest daughter of King Henry of France, as his wife, and for this purpose the Duke of Alba has been sent with full power to France to perform the marriage ceremony.[48]

The imagination of all the young ladies in Cremona must have been preoccupied with this fairy-tale couple. Philip was not an abstract entity, having passed through Cremona with an enormous entourage as crown prince in 1549, on his way across the Alps to Germany and Brussels. The city, which had been engaged in preparations for weeks, building triumphal arches, sent two hundred *cavalieri* to meet him. The city fathers, among them Amilcare, received him at the town gate. To everyone's amazement the prince did not look Spanish and daring, but was blond, reserved and very polite.[49] Sofonisba surely must have watched his arrival from a balcony.

One can easily imagine the excitement when, around June, two months after the peace proclamation, a letter arrived from the royal governor in Milan, the duke of Sessa, asking Amilcare if he would consent to send his daughter Sofonisba to Madrid to become the painting instructor for the young queen, Isabel. She would have the status of lady-in-waiting and receive all the honors and income of this prestigious appointment. The note probably was delivered by a close relative of the Anguissolas, Count Broccardo Persico, the owner of vast properties near Cremona and a member of the state council of Milan. A man who enjoyed the confidence of Philip II, Count Broccardo often was entrusted with diplomatic missions, later becoming general commissioner of the army. He conducted the initial negotiations with the Anguissolas on behalf of the duke of Sessa. The duke of Sessa was acting on behalf of the duke of Alba, who had met Isabel of Valois even before the king, on 22 June 1559 at the procuratorial wedding in Paris. The duke of Alba thus had the opportunity, probably at the king's request, to inquire about the future queen's hobbies, which might help make her life in Spain pleasant. When he found out that Isabel loved to draw, Alba, who had been governor of Milan for a brief period (1555-56), must have recalled the young, noble Italian who had stirred such interest with her paintings.

It remains unclear if the eager Amilcare contributed some effort of his own to introducing Sofonisba to Philip II. Sofonisba had painted a self-portrait for the king which was sent to Venice, where Titian's pupil Irene di Spilimbergo saw it and was deeply impressed. Was the picture meant to be taken to Spain by Sofonisba as a present for the king, after Titian had evaluated it? Did Amilcare hope to interest both Titian and Venice in his daughter at the same time? Or had it been painted earlier and sent with one of Titian's shipments of paintings for the king in Brussels, where he resided until September 1559, when he returned to Spain?

The honor bestowed on the family by the royal offer was immense. The favors that could be expected were tempting and a refusal would be very difficult to justify. On the one hand, although Amilcare saw his wishes fulfilled, he also had many doubts. Sofonisba herself, torn with conflicting emotions, certainly left the final decision up to her father, as any obedient daughter of that time would have done. The duke of Sessa allowed the family some time to consider their decision, and then invited them to Milan to discuss the matter. Count Broccardo accompanied Sofonisba and her parents, along with her sister Lucia. In Milan the duke of Sessa informed them of the details of the appointment, so they would have a better understanding of Sofonisba's future life. Sofonisba would receive a pension, actually a compensation for her parents, in addition to her salary as lady-in-waiting. On 6 September Amilcare finally gave his consent in writing. His touching letter to the king says in part:

The Duke of Sessa and Count Broccardo have asked me in Your Majesty's name to send my oldest daughter Sofonisba to serve our Highest Queen, Your Majesty's consort. As Your Majesty's devoted and obedient servant I oblige your wish, although it gives me great sorrow and deep unhappiness that my dearest daughter will be so far away, she whom we all love like life itself and whom we value above all else for her gifts and manners. But I take comfort in knowing that I have given her into the service of the greatest and best king, Catholic and Christian above all the others, and knowing also that Your Majesty's house is by reputation and in actuality run like a convent. Thanking the Lord for the opportunity to serve Your Majesty and regretting that due to my age and my responsibility for my other children I will not be able to accompany my daughter to serve Your Majesty in person as I have always wished I would be able to, I hereby conclude, so as not to keep Your Majesty any longer.[50]

There is no doubt that Sofonisba and the entire family made the best impression on the duke of Sessa, who was an intelligent and open-minded man. According to Pietro Paolo de Ribera,[51] the first and most reliable of Sofonisba's biographers, she was given a very generous allowance to purchase her traveling accoutrements.

P L A T E • 1 1

This portrait was originally identified as the representation of a physician, Pietro Maria, whom Giorgio Vasari had seen in Cremona in 1566. Later it was identified as Sofonisba's grandfather on her mother's side, *M.co Conte Pietro Martire, dottore.* Ultimately, the subject was convincingly identified by comparison with a portrait medal as the Cremonese physician Pietro Manna (F. Rossi 1985a, 351). An assumed relationship of this portrait of Pietro Manna by Lucia Anguissola to the portrait of a lady by Sofonisba in Berlin (Staatliche Museen Preubischer Kulturbesitz), which had been thought to be a pendant because of its almost identical dimensions, remains hypothetical. The portrait in Berlin is considered a portrait of Sofonisba's mother, Bianca Ponzoni Anguissola. If the Berlin portrait were a pendant to the portrait of Dr. Manna, it should logically depict Manna's wife and not Bianca Ponzoni. The Anguissola and Manna families were related, however . . . . Be that as it may, the idea of a painting competition between the sisters Lucia, who painted Dr. Manna, and Sofonisba, who painted the mother, cannot be excluded.

The psychological comprehension of the subject is impressive in this portrait. One sees the good-natured, keen, probing look and enlightened objectivity of a successful doctor, whose alert intellect captures every facet of the human condition. The blue, fur-trimmed robe, the snake and the armchair give equal weight to the person and to the composition of the picture, which must be one of the most successful portraits by Lucia.

A final detail is of interest. The "model" for the Aesculapian snake that is shown with the doctor is a yellow-green *coluber viridiflavus,* the snake most common in Lombardy (information kindly provided by Dr. H. Grillitsch, Naturhistorisches Museum, Vienna).

Exh. cat. Cremona 1994, no. 43 (A. Gilardi)

—*ALEXANDER WIED*

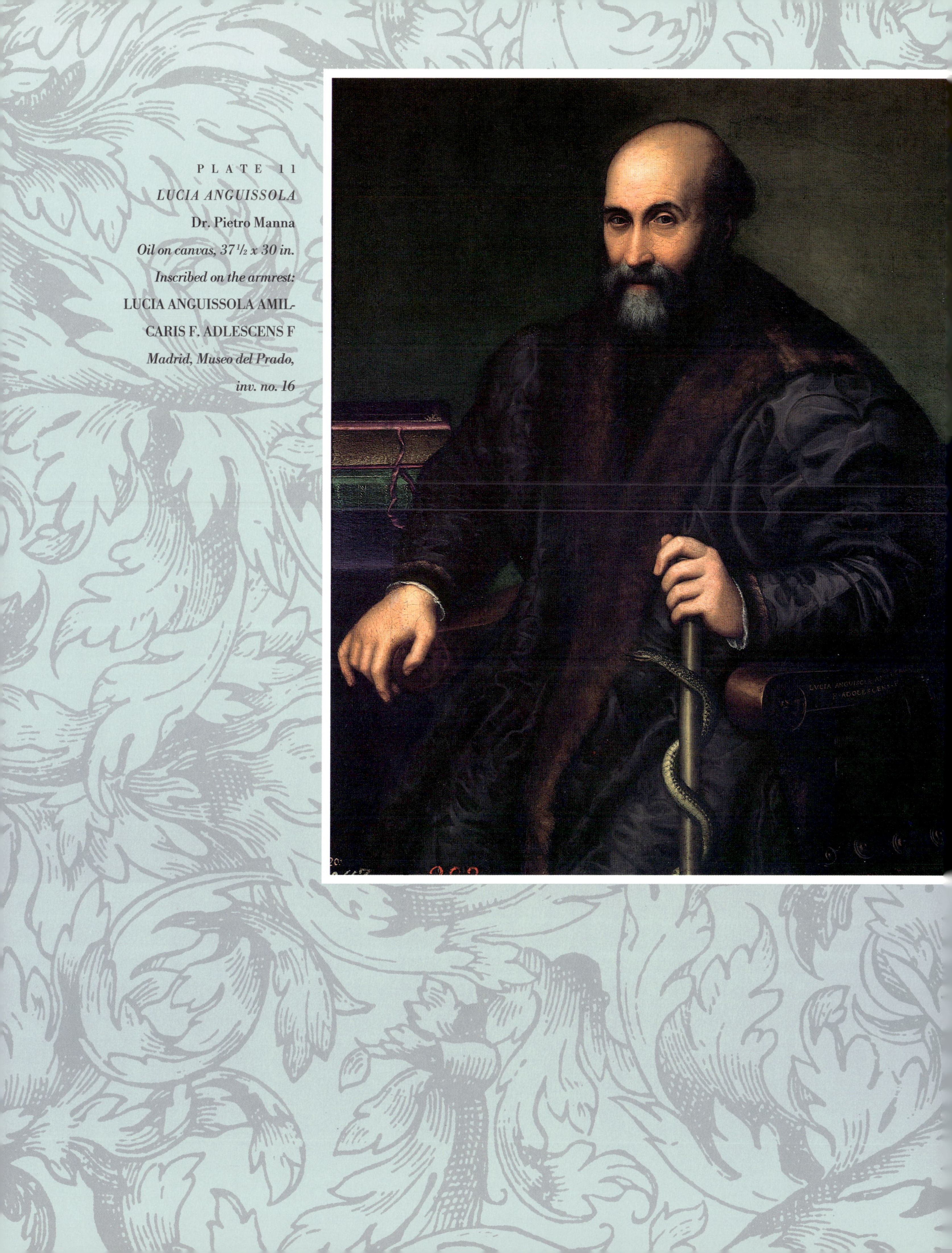

PLATE 11

LUCIA ANGUISSOLA

Dr. Pietro Manna

Oil on canvas, 37 1/2 x 30 in.

Inscribed on the armrest:

LUCIA ANGUISSOLA AMIL-CARIS F. ADLESCENS F

Madrid, Museo del Prado, inv. no. 16

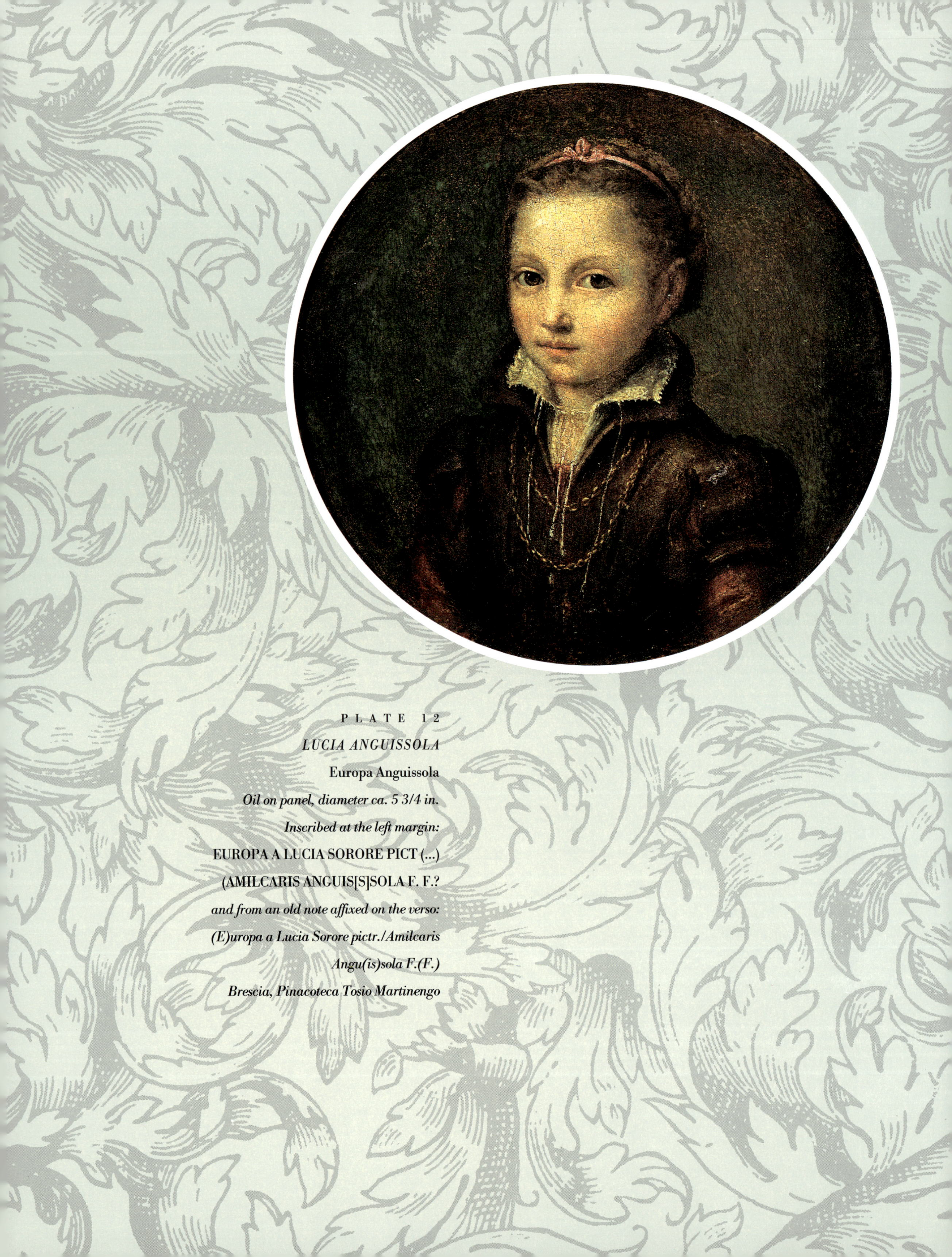

PLATE 12

LUCIA ANGUISSOLA

Europa Anguissola

Oil on panel, diameter ca. 5 3/4 in.

Inscribed at the left margin:

EUROPA A LUCIA SORORE PICT (...)

(AMILCARIS ANGUIS[S]SOLA F. F.?

and from an old note affixed on the verso:

(E)uropa a Lucia Sorore pictr./Amilcaris

Angu(is)sola F.(F.)

Brescia, Pinacoteca Tosio Martinengo

P L A T E ◆ 1 2

Europa's exact year of birth is not known, but it can be narrowed down to ca. 1548-49. The girl in the picture is eight to ten years old, dating the portrait to around 1556-58 (Gilardi in exh. ca. Cremona 1994, 76). Flavio Caroli (1973, 72) relates the tondo to Lucia's *Bianca Ponzoni Anguissola* in the Galleria Borghese in Rome and dates it to around 1555-58. A. Ghirardi (1992, 39) assumes a date of 1556-1558.

The fashionable details of the image—such as the dark jacket showing only a trace of the long-sleeved doublet at the neck, the laced and beribboned shirt collar and the gold necklaces—appear in other family portraits as well. In this painting the hair is held by a pink ribbon, highlighting the childlike aspect of the image and providing an accent to the portrait's red hues and the green background (frequently used by the Anguissolas).

Exh. cat. Cremona 1994, no. 44 (A. Gilardi)

—*ALEXANDER WIED*

The duke of Sessa gave the king an impression of his protégé, warmly recommended her to his care and reminded him to fulfill any obligations to her and her parents:

Sofonisba's great talents speak for themselves far better than any words I could use, as Your Majesty will see once she is before you. But so as not to leave out anything essential I would like to repeat that Sofonisba's parents, who love her very much—and with good reason—have only agreed to send her away to obey Your Majesty, and she has come here with the same goodwill, going so far away and leaving her parents, her siblings, her relatives, her home, and her country. I would like to recommend the parents and Sofonisba to Your Majesty, and Your Majesty should show them proof of Your favor. . . . Milan, 14 October 1559.[52]

In gratitude for the duke of Sessa's goodwill, the sisters each offered to paint his portrait. The duke was so enamored of Sofonisba's lifelike painting, and of the artist herself, that he gave her four bolts of precious brocade.

She also seems to have painted a picture of a *Small Boy with a Servant* (Saint Petersburg, The Hermitage)—perhaps one of the duke's young sons or that of another high-ranking nobleman. The importance she gives the figure of the nursemaid and the correspondence of the motif with a composition by Pieter Aertsen, which had been used by Giulio Campi, again show how much she was influenced by genre-like models.

In Milan two smaller self-portraits (Florence, Galleria degli Uffizi, and Milan, private collection) must have been painted[53] and certainly also another large, original work, her *Self-Portrait with Bernardino Campi* (Siena, Pinacoteca Nazionale), which was the result of a reunion with the much beloved old teacher, who had been living in Milan since he left Cremona. She combined his portrait with one of herself, as though he were painting her. His hand on her heart demonstrates his profound affection.

These self-portraits indicate a new self-confidence, and the smaller works feature a different, more court-oriented presentation. In the self-portrait with Campi the viewer may get an understanding of why Giovanni Paolo Lomazzo thought it seemed as though Titian were guiding her paintbrush.[54]

Meanwhile, a complete entourage had been assembled for her: two ladies, six servants and two gentlemen selected from among her relatives, who traveled in place of her father to "deliver" the young lady. One of them may have been Count Broccardo who, as we know from anecdotes passed down to us, also had developed a great affinity for Sofonisba.

In early November the group began the journey to Spain. From Milan to Genoa they traveled on horseback, the ladies at times in a sedan. In Genoa, Sofonisba set foot on a ship for the first time in her life. The ships were at sea for at least eight days and, because of the ever-present danger of pirate attacks, they had to stay close to the coast. We do not know if the ship was a freighter or a galley from the Spanish fleet, the Armada. In any case, life on board was rough and uncomfortable, and the party must have been relieved when they reached Barcelona in good health. Since they were important travelers, they must have been given a military escort—the countryside was not safe. When there were roads, they traveled by coach; in mountainous terrain, on horseback. They journeyed first through green Catalonia, then the Aragonese steppe and, finally, across the mountains of Castile to their interim destination of Guadalajara. There, at the magnificent palace of the duke of Infantado, one part of the court was waiting for the arrival of the young queen, while the other was on its way to the Pyrenees to meet her.

The Years in Spain: Sofonisba as Lady-in-Waiting and Painting Instructor to Isabel of Valois[55]

The king, according to Ribera, was very satisfied with Sofonisba's happy arrival in Guadalajara. She was greeted by Ruy Gómez da Silva, his chamberlain (the future duke of Eboli), and Diego de Córdoba, his equerry, who immediately dispensed the news of their safe arrival to Cremona.

Until the queen arrived at the end of January 1560, Sofonisba had time to acquaint herself with her new environment—a multilingual court, at which people from all over Europe were present. Sofonisba must have learned some Spanish in Milan. Very soon she must have called on the most important lady of the court, the princess-widow of Portugal, Doña Juana, who had been the Spanish regent until the recent return of Philip II from the Netherlands.

On 28 January Isabel of Valois entered Guadalajara and established herself with her huge French household, and even larger royal Spanish household, at the immense palace of the Infantado, where the attendants of Infanta Juana and those of the king already resided. One can imagine the bustle at the palace and in town.

The wedding took place on the day after Isabel arrived, 29 January. After an additional marriage ceremony, performed by the cardinal of Burgos, the entire court attended Mass and watched the public banquet of the royal persons. That night there was a ball. This must have been the first occasion for everyone to notice the young Italian lady, and all eyes were fixed on her. She evidently was not only an excellent dancer but also moved around the court with self-possession and ease. The envoy of the duke of Mantua, Girolamo Neri, describes the big day to his master and relates this incident:

On the night of the wedding, the king proposed to dance a galliard and since no one wanted to begin, Signore Ferrante Gonzaga was the first to dance; he asked the young Cremonese who paints and who came here to stay with the queen, which opened the way for many who danced after them.[56]

This young member of the Gonzaga household did the honors for his country and at the same time introduced Sofonisba to the court. During the last dance a torch was passed around. The ladies and gentlemen took turns inviting each other to dance, dancing and passing the torch along. When Sofonisba received the torch from the Prince de La Roche, the queen's cousin, she, being more worldly and more liberally raised than the young Spanish ladies-in-waiting, asked the master of the house, the duke of Infantado, for a dance. She danced with the duke and then passed the torch to the king himself. Philip II, who must have been charmed by her grace and self-confidence, honored her with a very deep bow. With that, her position at court was established.[57] Her debut at court could not have been more favorable for the young artist. These incidents confirm what her relationship with the duke of Sessa and Count Broccardo in Milan has already established, that the fame of Sofonisba's beauty and poise was not just meaningless flattery—she truly was a woman of great appeal.

On 4 February 1560 the court started on the journey to the former capital, Toledo, via Alcalá and Madrid. The old residence in Toledo would serve as temporary quarters until the palace in Madrid, the future residence, was completed. Triumphal arches, laden with humanist allegories, had been set up in the old university town of Alcalá. The queen rode into Madrid on her horse under a canopy, accompanied by all the young ladies in her entourage. After a long triumphal procession, she was received in the Alcázar (castle) by the king, the infanta, Doña Juana, and the grandees of Spain. They spent a few days in the palace in temporarily appointed quarters, and attended tournaments and bullfights. On the way to Toledo the crowds, lined up along the route, jubilantly greeted the queen as "Isabel de la paz," the peace bearer.

The old, distinguished capital of Toledo received the queen with elation and great pomp on 12 February 1560. The whole city was decorated with triumphal arches, fountains, monuments and other wooden structures. Here, too, the young queen and her ladies had to endure a reception that lasted many hours.

Sofonisba must have compared the old-fashioned, dark walls of the Alcázar with the modern, spacious, bright, cheerful, comfortable Italian palaces which she knew. Her well-balanced personality and tact assisted her in winning the trust of the childlike queen, then only fourteen, who immediately began to draw with her. Sofonisba's experiences with her young sisters were helpful in this regard. When the French ambassador, Limoges, visited the queen's quarters one week later, he surprised both of them at work. Isabel was so proud of her new ability that she began to sketch a portrait right before his eyes. He writes to Catherine de' Medici that it was uncanny how much her daughter had learned in such a short period of time from an Italian lady that the king had commissioned to instruct her. Limoges had taken the drawing and was sending it to her. He also asked Catherine de' Medici whether she recognized who it was—the queen most likely had made a sketch of him.

During these exercises Sofonisba and her pupil must have sketched one another to combine work and pleasure. Up to this point Sofonisba had painted no large portrait of the queen. Isabel was soon portrayed by Alonso Sánchez Coello (Vienna, Kunsthistorisches Museum) and Anthonis Mor (Antonio Moro - copy in Madrid, Collection Varez Fina), the two skilled court painters. Sofonisba herself held back, following the old adage that the right time has to come for a beautiful portrait. In both paintings the queen appears tired and worn, and must indeed not have been an attractive model this first year. When the fatigue caused by her travels had just passed and life in the open air—horseback riding, excursions and hunting expeditions in the company of her ladies, the young Don Juan, Don Carlos and the Prince of Eboli—seemed to have strengthened her, an attack of chicken pox struck her down again. During her convalescence in the cold months of winter, the queen eagerly pursued her studies with Sofonisba.

In May 1561 the court moved to Madrid. Here painting was resumed, as recalled by Madame de Vineux, Keeper of the Wardrobe for Catherine de' Medici, in September: "She spends most of her time painting, which gives her great joy. I also believe that if she continues in this fashion she will become as masterful as her teacher, who is one of the best in the world."[58]

What did Sofonisba do with her time when she was not instructing the queen? There were sixteen young ladies-in-waiting, who lived together in a boarding school environment. Five were Spanish, daughters of the finest families in the country, and six were from the French high aristocracy. Sofonisba, whose family of low Italian nobility from the merchant class officially was held equal to the others' but whose circumstances were so much more modest, must often have felt it necessary to evade indiscreet questions. Between the Spanish and the French girls there were sometimes small jealousies, which finally became such an issue between two of them that the French lady-in-waiting had to leave. Sofonisba was caught in the middle between these groups, which may at times have been an advantage and at other times a disadvantage.

These fine young women were carefully protected by a type of governess, the *guardamenor*, who watched over them with eagle eyes. According to the king's rules for the queen's household, she had to lock the doors and windows of the sleeping quarters at night, make sure that candles were always burning in the halls and, above all, monitor arrivals and departures at all times. She also presided over the joint dinner the ladies shared, ensuring that there was no unruly behavior and that everyone observed proper manners. The king's rules also stated that the young ladies could only eat what was served, being given different foods only in case of illness. They were not allowed more than one personal maidservant, even if they paid for additional service themselves. They were permitted one groom to care for the riding horses and run errands. These rules, obviously based on past experience, must have been meant to discourage too much luxury among the young ladies and to prevent the chaos of too many personal servants running too many private errands.

There seems to have been enough attention paid to the entertainment of the ladies-in-waiting, however. Their life was a succession of parties, carnivals, hunting expeditions, theater performances, dances and musical performances. The young ladies themselves participated in the carnival and the theater, naturally without the company of men. The presence of gentlemen was, however, unrestricted at any of the public events, for example the king's public banquet. There, the ladies perched on pillows alongside the walls of the assembly rooms and the gentlemen stood next to them and entertained them. Ribera describes the scene:

Since Sofonisba was much favored by both majesties, many Spanish and Italian gentlemen courted her, and so her fame spread so much due to her inner and outer virtues that she, just like the other high-ranking ladies of the queen's attendance, was equally well regarded by everyone.[59]

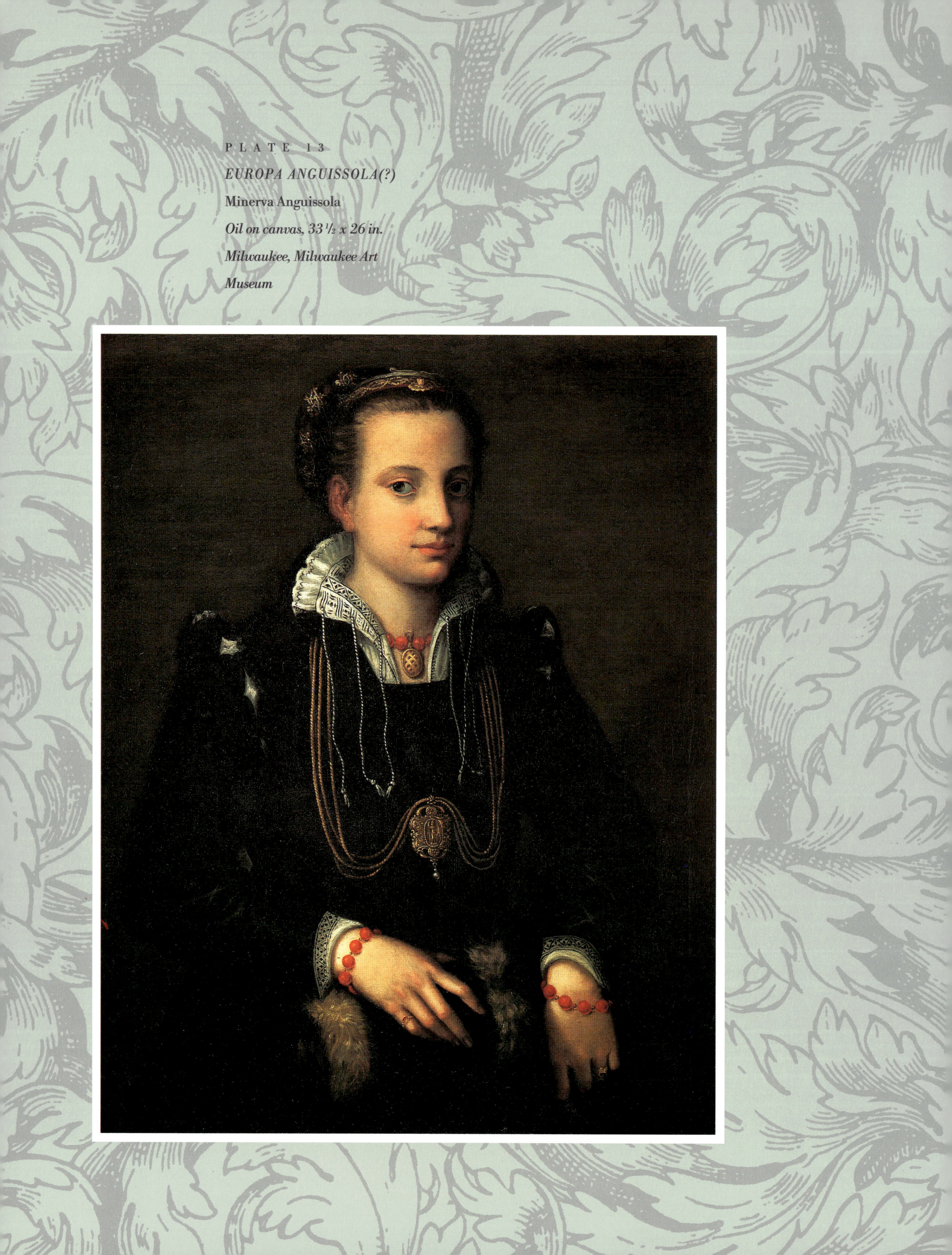

PLATE 13

EUROPA ANGUISSOLA(?)

Minerva Anguissola

Oil on canvas, 33 ½ x 26 in.

Milwaukee, Milwaukee Art Museum

When acquired in 1931, this work was accompanied by an appraisal by Voss of 1928, who declared the picture a self-portrait by Sofonisba. The identification of the subject as Minerva was made by A. Ghirardi (1992, 35-41), based on the medallion with an armed Minerva, which undoubtedly alludes to her first name and her erudition.

The picture in three-quarter profile presents a standing young lady, her hands resting on a fur-trimmed muff. Her hairstyle, including the hair ornamentation, is artful, the red coral at the neck and wrists accentuates her diaphanous skin. While the catalogue in Milwaukee (Fernández Gimenez 1986, 28) assumes a date of 1558-59, Ghirardi (1992, 40) suggests 1564 as the date of origin, the year of Minerva's death. The work thus would be a portrait in memoriam. This would better explain the statuesque rendering of the subject, which then would reflect not only observance of the rules of Spanish etiquette but also the necessity to rely on drawings sent by her sisters to inform Sofonisba of the adult Minerva's appearance.

Maria Kusche, however, has rightfully doubted the attribution of the portrait to Sofonisba because of the obvious stylistic deviations. She has suggested Europa Anguissola as the artist (Kusche, 1995, fnt. 31; about Europa, see A. Gilardi in exh. cat. Cremona 1994, 74).

Exh. cat. Cremona 1994, no. 22 (R. Sacchi)

—*ALEXANDER WIED*

P L A T E • 1 3

The financial aspects of Sofonisba's life now began to stabilize. From June 1560 onward she received her "ordinary" salary as a lady-in-waiting: 100 ducats per year (as a foreigner, she was given the same as the French ladies and one quarter more than the Spanish). In addition, there were "extraordinary" allowances, such as a salary and pension for her two servants, a lady's maid and a groom, as well as money for the washerwoman, for candles and for horse or mule feed. The "ordinary" payments always were only payments *a conto* (on account), for the most urgent necessities. Often the irregularly padded royal coffers ran out of funds entirely, and the debts of the treasurers to the young ladies grew. For the Spanish ladies, whose parents most often formed part of the court, this was no problem. It was also not a problem for the daughters of powerful French families, who were able to support themselves with private funds. Sofonisba, however, had no such backing. She once had to ask the duke of Alba himself for help, and several times sought assistance from the king.

On 1 July 1561 a promise was fulfilled that probably had been made in Milan: Sofonisba received a lifelong pension of 200 ducats, raised from taxes on the wines produced in Cremona and payable to her father. This pension also arrived only irregularly, due to bureaucratic obstacles. The money, a vital source of income for her family, kept Sofonisba under obligation to the king.

Once in Madrid in 1561, Sofonisba finally was able to resume her artistic activities, and must also have been given a small studio. During this first year in Madrid, one picture followed another. As we know from a letter by Sofonisba to Bernardino Campi of the same year, the queen also demanded her attention, and she complained that she hardly had any time.[60] On the one hand, Sofonisba had to juggle her self-imposed demands for quality in her profession and those of her environment. On the other, she also needed to meet the demands that her high rank as lady-in-waiting to the queen required. Thus her life was not easy. She could not openly compete with the court painters who, despite any fondness that the king had for them, were still primarily seen as craftsmen. This must have been the reason that, while at court, she never signed her paintings, as she had done formerly in Italy. She also never received any monetary compensation for her works of art; had it been offered, she would have refused it—only gifts or other favors were acceptable. She certainly had contact with the court artists and other Italian artists, such as Giovanni Battista Castello and Pompeo Leoni. She also must have known Sánchez Coello's daughter Isabel, who painted and, evidently, copied her father's paintings in miniature. Sofonisba also must have studied the portraits themselves in the royal treasury and the galleries very carefully, for the influence of these pictures resonates in her own work.

Sofonisba's special position at court poses a problem for interested posterity, as the Spanish paintings are unsigned and no payment receipts exist to document her authorship. Her paintings, thus, quickly disappeared among the oeuvre of the other court painters. To be able to rediscover and reattribute her Spanish work, the fame of which was passed down only through old treatises on art, a wide variety of documentary sources and stylistic features from extant portraits of the period had to be brought to bear.

Sofonisba's first portrait of the queen, Isabel of Valois, "with the flea-fur" (a flea-attracting marten-pelt which protected the ladies against these insects), which delighted the court, was painted in Madrid in 1561. Isabel by now had recovered and grown into her new role. What she lacked in beauty she made up for with liveliness and French charm. For this formal portrait Sofonisba used for the first time the court model—a sine qua non for depictions of the royal family. Although she chose the large format for her first painting, not the three-quarter format, she completed the task with characteristic flair. Unfortunately, neither the original version with full-size figures nor the later version in three-quarter size have survived. The full-figure composition exists only as a copy by Rubens (formerly London, Morris Collection; now Toledo, private collection), which he must have produced for the duke of Mantua during his stay in Madrid in 1603. There is also a copy of the shortened version, probably by Juan Pantoja de la Cruz (plate 14). We only gather from a small, signed replica made by Sofonisba herself in her later years (plate 16) how delicate and expressive the smiling face in the original painting was. Sofonisba sent one copy of this first picture to Pope Pius IV. Her letter to him dated 16 September 1561 clearly shows how much she wanted to do justice to the personality of her subject:

If it were possible to demonstrate before the eyes of Your Holiness with the brush the beauty of the soul of this illustrious queen, Your Holiness could not see anything more wonderful. But in those aspects that art is able to render I have not neglected to the best of my ability to show Your Holiness the truth (il vero).

This portrait already hints at how Sofonisba's work would progress in Spain. The agility of the figure and the sweetness of the countenance were new in the art of the Spanish court. Here Sofonisba's work departed from that of the great Spanish-Portuguese realist Sánchez Coello and the Netherlander Anthonis Mor, the master of courtly elegance and dignity. She begins from a very different vantage point than the court painters. Sofonisba and the queen had developed a friendship, and the painter wishes to convey the kindness, warmth and congeniality that her subject radiates. To do justice to the large formal portrait pattern is only a secondary objective. Sofonisba based this portrait on pictures she found at the court, especially the ones by Titian and Mor, combining them with impressions from Cremona. Her sense of beauty, her interest in the subject's personality, the greater freedom of posture and the softer treatment of the surface and outline made the painting a great success. The version shown here became famous not only in Italy, because a copy had been sent to the pope, it also became the most frequently copied portrait in Spain. Sofonisba was asked to make a replica of the three-quarter figure for the king's sister, Infanta Juana, a copy of which Philip II hung in the portrait gallery at the Prado. The full-length original was kept in the royal treasury, among the other most highly prized paintings.

Next Sofonisba painted a portrait of Infanta Juana, as indicated by Sofonisba's

PLATE • 14

The Treaty of Cateau-Cambrésis, negotiated between Philip II of Spain and Henry II of France to end decades of hostilities between the two neighboring countries, was sealed with a political marriage. On January 29, 1560, Philip II married his third wife, Isabel of Valois, the daughter of Henry II and Catherine de' Medici, born in 1545.

Sofonisba Anguissola was called to the Spanish court in 1559 to serve Isabel, then barely fifteen, as lady-in-waiting and to teach her to draw. One of her duties at court also was to create portraits of the young queen. Her first painting was a large, full-length representative portrait painted at least two versions, one for the king himself (Kusche 1992a, 15) and the other for Pope Pius IV. There was an additional smaller version in three-quarter size for the Princess Juana, sister of Philip II. These paintings, listed in contemporary documents as Sofonisba's works, are lost and exist today only as copies. The extant versions and the ones mentioned in inventories, as well as the lost examples, all have one peculiar feature—a marten pelt set in precious stones and fastened to a chain, used as an accessory by ladies to attract fleas and prevent them from molesting the owner of the fur.

The three-quarter portrait painted by Sofonisba for Princess Juana is described in detail in the inventory of her paintings at the convent of the Las Descalzas Reales in Madrid. Alonso Sánchez Coello must have painted his example after this version, which was intended for the portrait gallery at the El Pardo palace (Kusche 1989, 400; Kusche 1991a, 101; Kusche 1991b, 273; Kusche 1992c, 11). When the palace burned down in 1604, the painting was destroyed and later replaced with a copy made by Juan Pantoja de la Cruz, court painter to Philip III, in 1610 (Kusche 1964, 107). In all likelihood this painting is identical with the one exhibited here, which came from the old royal collection and is the most beautiful and best preserved of all extant copies (exh. cat. Madrid 1990, no. 6; see Garrido, exh. cat. Madrid 1990, 231).

Exh. cat. Cremona 1994, 97, 127, cat. no. 23 (M. Kusche)

—KARL SCHÜTZ

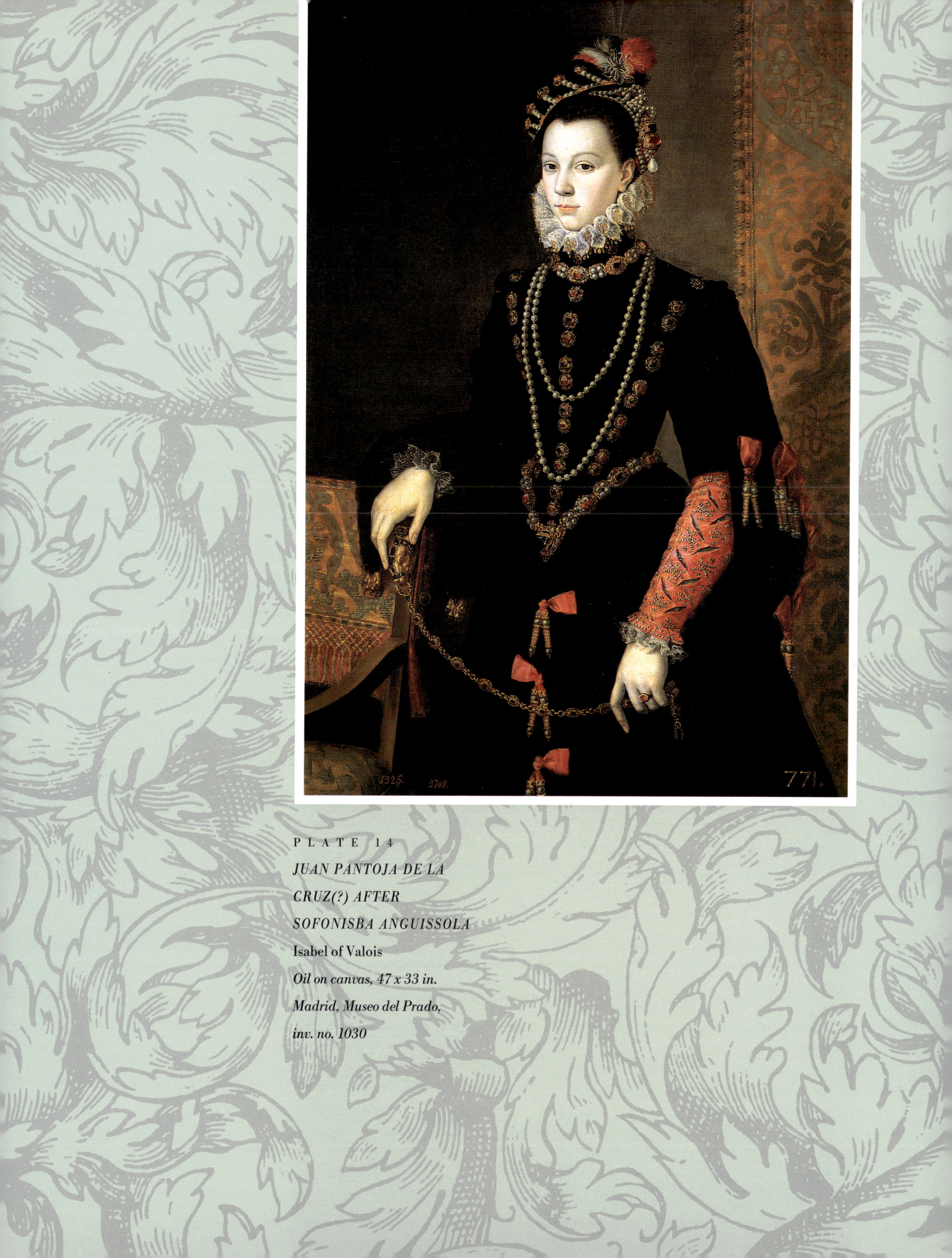

PLATE 14

JUAN PANTOJA DE LA CRUZ(?) AFTER SOFONISBA ANGUISSOLA

Isabel of Valois

Oil on canvas, 47 x 33 in.

Madrid, Museo del Prado, inv. no. 1030

P L A T E • 1 5

Just like Sofonisba's first *Isabel of Valois* of 1561 with the marten fur (compare plate 14), this full-length portrait of the queen adheres to the stringent rules of Spanish court portraiture, with which the artist was fully familiar. The queen holds a miniature portrait of Philip II in her right hand, obviously intending to show it to the viewer and thereby demonstrating that the miniature is not just a decorative element. A portrait of the Infanta Juana attributed to Sánchez Coello (Bilbao, Museo de Bellas Artes) with the miniature portrait of Philip II presents her in her capacity as the regent of Spain on behalf of the king.

The portrait of the king held by Queen Isabel may indicate that she functions as his substitute as well. The occasion may possibly be the meeting that took place in Bayonne in the summer of 1565. Spain wanted to solicit a commitment from the allied French against the Protestant Huguenots. Catherine de' Medici participated in this meeting as regent, on behalf of her son Charles IX. Her daughter Isabel of Valois, the Spanish queen, represented King Philip II.

This portrait was earlier attributed to Juan Pantoja de la Cruz and traditionally has been considered a copy, probably after a lost version by Sánchez Coello (cat. Madrid 1963, 617), until it was determined to be an original work by Sofonisba (Kusche 1964, 193). The new attribution, supported by an examination of the painting technique and an x-ray (Garrido in exh. cat. Madrid 1990, 229), is now generally accepted (exh. cat. Madrid 1990, no. 5).

Exh. cat. Cremona 1994, 99, 131, no. 24 (M. Kusche)

—KARL SCHÜTZ

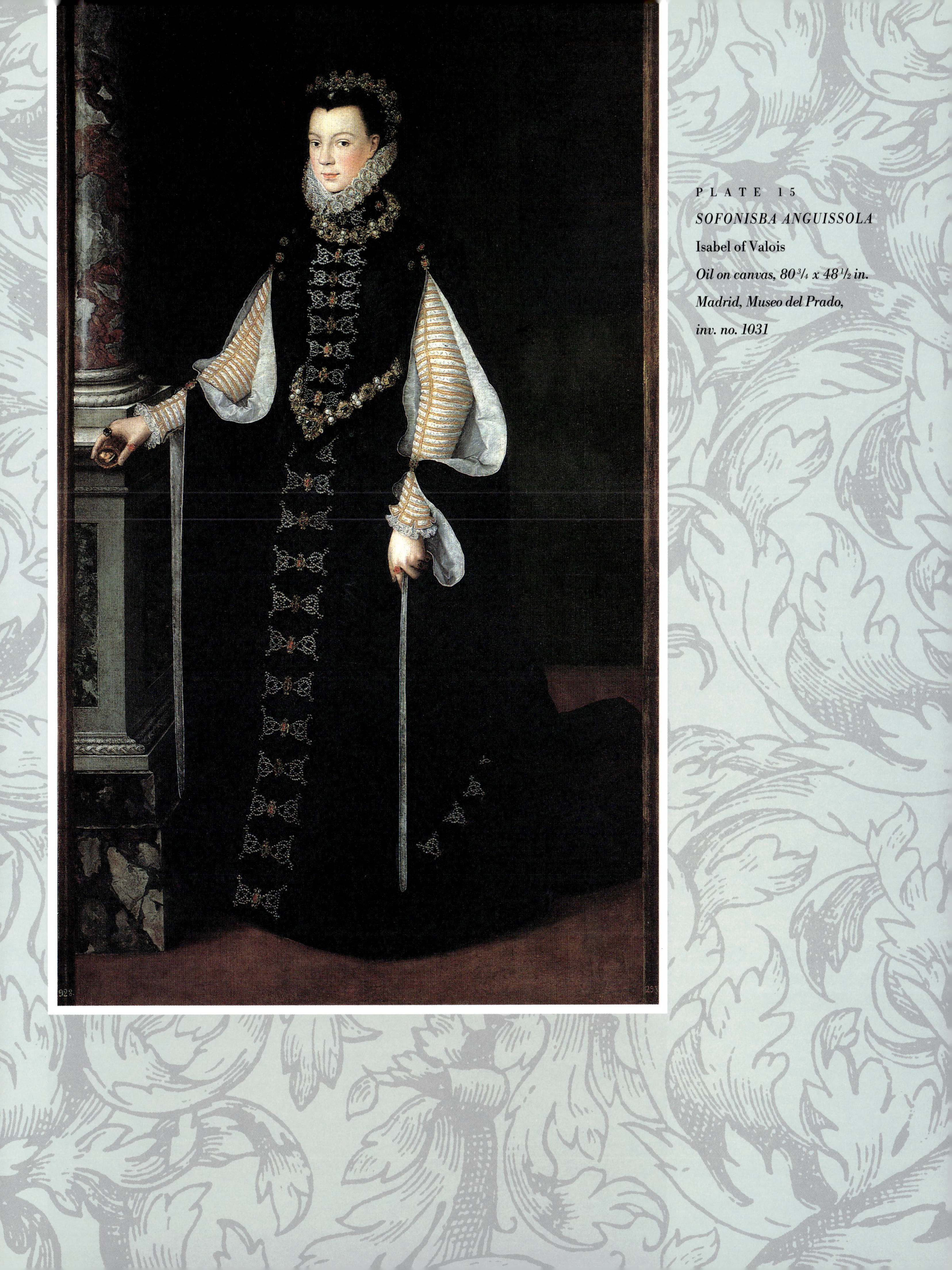

PLATE 15

SOFONISBA ANGUISSOLA

Isabel of Valois

Oil on canvas, 80 3/4 x 48 1/2 in.

Madrid, Museo del Prado,

inv. no. 1031

previously mentioned letter to Bernardino Campi in October 1561. In this case, the painting was intended for the pope from the beginning. Juana, the widowed princess of Portugal, had retreated to the Clarissan convent, Las Descalsas Reales, which she had founded, but without becoming a nun. Whenever she was not needed at court, she devoted her life wholly to her religious endeavors. *Juana of Austria* (frontispiece) must be identical with the work sent to the pope. Here a little girl—a future nun, with three roses in her hand, for obedience, chastity and poverty—accompanies the princess. The figure of the girl is reminiscent of her childhood images from Cremona. The figure of Juana shows very similar characteristics to the first portrait of Queen Isabel and also the following one (plates 14 and 15). In comparison with the work of the court painters, also this painting of Juana shows a much stronger emphasis on beauty, with its diffused shadows and transitions, as well as its fluid contour. The accentuation of the personal circumstances—here allusions to Juana's religious life, such as the little future novice, a window that shows only the sky, the complete lack of worldly luxury—also points to Sofonisba as the originator.

Alessandro Farnese (Dublin, National Gallery of Ireland) must have been painted that same year. It apparently was copied the following year in a fresco at the palace of his uncle, Cardinal Farnese, in Caprarola, which was intended for the glorification of the house of Farnese. Alessandro, son of Margaret of Parma, was raised at the court of Philip II. Sofonisba perhaps had already met the boy in Parma. After her arrival in Toledo in 1560, the two, as the only young Italians, had had occasion to talk more often and refresh their memories of Parma.

The composition of this work is based on a painting of the prince by Anthonis Mor made in Brussels in 1557 (Parma, Galleria Nazionale). Here the model is transformed in the same manner as in the two previously painted portraits of the queen and Infanta Juana. The awkward, reticent boy by Mor turns into a self-assured, graceful youth. Mainly it is its resemblance with Sofonisba's *Self-Portrait* of three years later (Chantilly, Musée Condé), particularly in the treatment of the face, the outline, shadowing and the tonal variation of the colors which assure that the portrait of Alessandro Farnese belongs to her. The Farnese portrait resembles also the well documented *Don Carlos* (copy, Madrid, formerly Colección Bauza, today lost), particularly in the volume of the figure and the extraordinary splendor of the clothing. This painting of Alessandro also was very well received, as its inclusion in the fresco in Caprarola demonstrates. Cardinal Farnese evidently did not mind that Alessandro actually had not been more than five years of age at the time of the historical scene represented in the fresco.

At about this period Sofonisba met another Italian prince, the son of Cosimo I de' Medici, the future Francesco de' Medici. Like many other Italian princes, he had been sent to the Spanish court on a diplomatic mission and had been in Spain in 1562/63. In later years he alluded to this meeting and evidently had fond memories of the painter. It is also possible that Sofonisba worked for him.

Despite much work, these first years of successes, spent in the benevolent care of the royal couple, must have been happy ones for Sofonisba. The queen overwhelmed her with gifts, "once a valuable dress, once a jewel-encrusted necklace, pearls, or other royal presents," as recounted by Ribera, "so that she was always opulently dressed and adorned." Her previously mentioned *Self-Portrait* of 1564 (Chantilly, Musée Condé) reveals her new appearance, appropriate for the Spanish court, as well as her maturity and self-assurance. She wears a black velvet dress with gold embroidery, similar to the one worn by the queen in the replica of her first portrait (plate 16). Surely Isabel passed down her own dresses to her ladies-in-waiting. A precious intertwined gold chain set with diamonds hangs around Sofonisba's neck. Her hair is arranged in small, soft curls. The portrait must have been made before the news of her sister Minerva's death arrived that same year. Minerva died at barely twenty years of age.

The court went on many brief outings, on which the ladies accompanied the queen on horseback, in the coach and, sometimes, in the sedan. Royal country estates were located all around Madrid. The Casa de Campo and El Pardo were both destinations for such excursions. Further south was Aranjuez; Valsaín stood in the mountains to the north. The convent and palace of Escorial were under construction.

In 1565 a big journey was undertaken. Isabel of Valois, accompanied by the duke of Alba, was sent by Philip II on a diplomatic mission to Bayonne. She was to meet her mother, Catherine de' Medici, and admonish her, in the name of the king, to take a more decisive position against the Huguenots and to be more diligent in meeting the conditions of the Council of Trent.

Sofonisba painted her second full-length *Isabel of Valois* (plate 15) quite obviously for this occasion. Here the queen, as the representative of Philip II, holds the king's portrait in her hand. The same gesture can be seen in other portraits of royal ladies of that time and has similar symbolic meaning. Sofonisba painted this work as an official court portrait, adhering to the Spanish court school much more closely than she had in the previous ones. It is more closely related to examples by Titian and Mor. Here the subject is no longer a cheerful young girl, but the queen of Spain. It can be assumed that the picture was intended as a present for Catherine de' Medici, but perhaps had not been completed in time and remained behind in Spain. Sofonisba enjoyed great success in Bayonne. The negotiations between the Spaniards and the French were accompanied by grand celebrations and festivities. Sofonisba won a beautiful medallion, one of the six prizes awarded for virtue. Pierre de Bourdeilles Brantome noted that the queen seemed to prefer one particular lady to most of the Spanish and many of the French ladies-in-waiting: "an Italian lady, a young woman from Cremona, beautiful, virtuous, and kind, with the best talents, and especially capable of painting well and portraying from nature."

On her return from this trip Sofonisba must have found notification of a second death. Lucia, her sister and former student, who had become a talented and promising painter in her own right, died in 1565, just over twenty years of age. Sofonisba must have grieved much, experiencing two consecutive losses in such a short time.

Just before or just after her return from France, Sofonisba painted the *Philip II* (plate 17) which Ribera mentions. It exists today as a pendant to the portrait of Philip II's next wife, Anne of Austria, but the features of the king do not bear the marks of the years following this next marriage. In this portrait the king's face, later usually melancholy, is still smooth and without wrinkles. He has a relaxed, serene, content expression. In fact, an x-ray has revealed that the king originally was portrayed with his hand on his chest, without the cape and rosary. His posture and clothing were thus less severe and more in keeping with a youthful, happier era. The portrait must have been created in the years before the deaths of Isabel and Don Carlos in 1568.

With this portrait, Sofonisba masterfully achieved a personal description of the king, simultaneously expressing all her reverence for him. No other portrait of Philip II compares in that respect. The facial features are reminiscent of works by Pompeo Leoni. It can be assumed that the artist was acquainted with Leoni, who also owned one of her paintings, which is mentioned in his will. With the portrait of the king, Sofonisba returned to the format of her Italian works. Here the dual influence of Italy is especially apparent: the soft, Correggio-like treatment of the flesh, which recalls her training with Bernardino Gatti, and the miniaturist rendering of details, which, nevertheless, never seems dry or pedantic, taken from Clovio. The spare coloration of the clothing against an olive-green background is also familiar from her Italian paintings. Philip II's portrait would become the one painting of him most frequently reproduced. The later addition of the rosary and the severe cape, and above all its wide-ranging distribution in the form of hard etchings, subsequently changed its character.

Around 1567 another one of Sofonisba's famous paintings must have been produced, that of Don Carlos. Unfortunately, the original is lost. The prince liked it so much that he ordered thirteen copies from Sánchez Coello and six additional versions from another artist. Only four remain today, among them only one of acceptable quality (Madrid, formerly Colección Bauza, today lost). No wonder the prince preferred this portrait to the highly realistic ones by the court painter. The magnificent garment, already praised by Ribera and exactly described in Sánchez Coello's bills, hides the physical defects that the degenerate, hunchbacked prince suffered. Sofonisba transformed him into an acceptable successor to the throne, and he reciprocated with an acknowledgment of gratitude and a valuable ring.

At the end of 1566 the palace experienced great joy and hope: the queen was finally pregnant. Just before the delivery in Valsaín, Isabel took time to write her will, which bespeaks her warm relationship with her ladies. Leaving a bequest to each, she urges the king to carry out her wishes in the event of her death and to take care of the ladies in every conceivable way. In most cases, the legacies are contributions to their dowries. Sofonisba is the third lady listed, immediately following the Spanish and French favorites. The queen's will entitles her to 3,000 ducats and one bolt of brocade for a bed.

The baby, born without difficulties, was a girl—Isabel Clara Eugenia, future sovereign of the Netherlands. The following year a sister was born—Catalina Micaela, later duchess of Savoy. Both were robust, intelligent and healthy, the only ones of Philip's children without genetic defects.

The young queen died unexpectedly during her third pregnancy in October 1568. The bereavement of her young companions was indescribable. Philip II fell into a deep depression. Bernardo Maschi, who was always on the scene as the envoy of Francesco Maria della Rovere, duke of Urbino, wrote on the day of her death: "Sofonisba says she does not want to go on living."

The Spanish Years: Sofonisba Teacher of the Infantas and Lady-in-Waiting to Infanta Juana and Queen Anne[61]

In late October 1568, Maschi wrote to his master, the duke of Urbino, that the queen's French ladies were returning to France, the Spanish ones were being sent home and that Sofonisba might perhaps join the princess, Doña Juana. The same day Raimond de Fourqueveaux, the French ambassador, described the situation at the palace to Catherine de' Medici. The princess was ill, the small infantas were well, the duchess of Alba (the *Camarera Mayor* or Chief Lady of the Household to the late queen, who was also responsible for the little infantas) was still running the entire household like the mother superior of a convent. During this transition Sofonisba could be seen rushing back and forth between the Alcázar and the monastery-palace Las Descalzas Reales to care for the departing companions and the sick Infanta Juana.

To fulfill his special responsibility for the destitute Sofonisba according to the wishes of his deceased queen, the king very soon initiated the necessary steps to marry her to a Spanish nobleman. The artist enjoyed his complete confidence; her talents, her character, her education made her an ideal teacher for the infantas, and he wanted to keep her at court. But Sofonisba, exhausted by the events that had taken place, was homesick for her family and begged him to let her marry in Italy. Philip, always sympathetic toward people who enjoyed his trust, withdrew his plan.

The search for an Italian husband was handed over to Diego de Córdoba, the same nobleman who had once met the arriving Sofonisba in Guadalajara. His task turned out to be more difficult than expected. At first an attempt was made to settle her near Cremona. Diego de Córdoba asked Count Broccardo for help. The good count's efforts proved to be in vain, however, since the gentlemen he approached were afraid not to be able to accommodate the whims of a spoiled lady-in-waiting. Sofonisba also was no longer very young. Diego de Córdoba reported on the situation to Cardinal Espinosa, the president of the royal council. The report, dating to about 1569, is not without its humor:

Ercules Vizconti, master of two towns in the state of Milan and one in Piacenza, who has a good fortune and once was interested in the lady in question, says he no longer is and marriage is out of the question.

Cesar Casato from Novara, who is of very noble and powerful descent and has a pension of 6,000 ducats and a number of soldiers, and is highly recommended for his good reputation and the many friends he has everywhere . . . would like to marry the Sofonisba, if he were given the governance of Novara. This was refused, . . . but his final condition is the governance of Novara and a squadron of soldiers, . . . because he knows what His Majesty usually gives the ladies-in-waiting. His greatest concern is honor, more

P L A T E ◆ 1 6

This painting is the only one of the court portraits that is signed. The signature shows Sofonisba's last name from her second marriage to Orazio Lomellini. The painting and its signature doubtless date from the same time, which must be after 1580, presumably around 1590, when the artist had already been living in Genoa for several years.

It was earlier believed that the portrait represented the Infanta Isabel Clara Eugenia and could have been created for the occasion of her journey to the Netherlands in 1599, when she stopped over in Genoa (Klauner 1961, 148). But at that time she was thirty-three years old. The infanta does, however, seem noticeably younger here. In fact, the portrait does not depict Isabel Clara Eugenia but rather her mother, Isabel of Valois, long deceased at the time the portrait was painted. This is confirmed by a comparison with Sofonisba's portrait of her from 1561, which is only extant as a copy (plate 14) (Kusche 1964, 108). The portrait blends elements taken from both the full-length and the three-quarter-length version of the queen's portrait of 1561. Sofonisba Anguissola may have painted the bust-length version for an unknown patron, perhaps after a version in small format that she had in her possession.

Parts of the portrait are in poor condition today. The background, in particular, is heavily damaged, although the paint layers on the face and the dress are better preserved. Restoration was only performed to maintain the current condition. A conscious effort was made to avoid retouching areas lacking paint by inpainting; only a light transition between painted areas and those areas where the paint had disappeared was completed, for the optical coherence of the composition.

Exh. cat. Cremona 1994, 140, no. 29 (M. Kusche)

— *KARL SCHÜTZ*

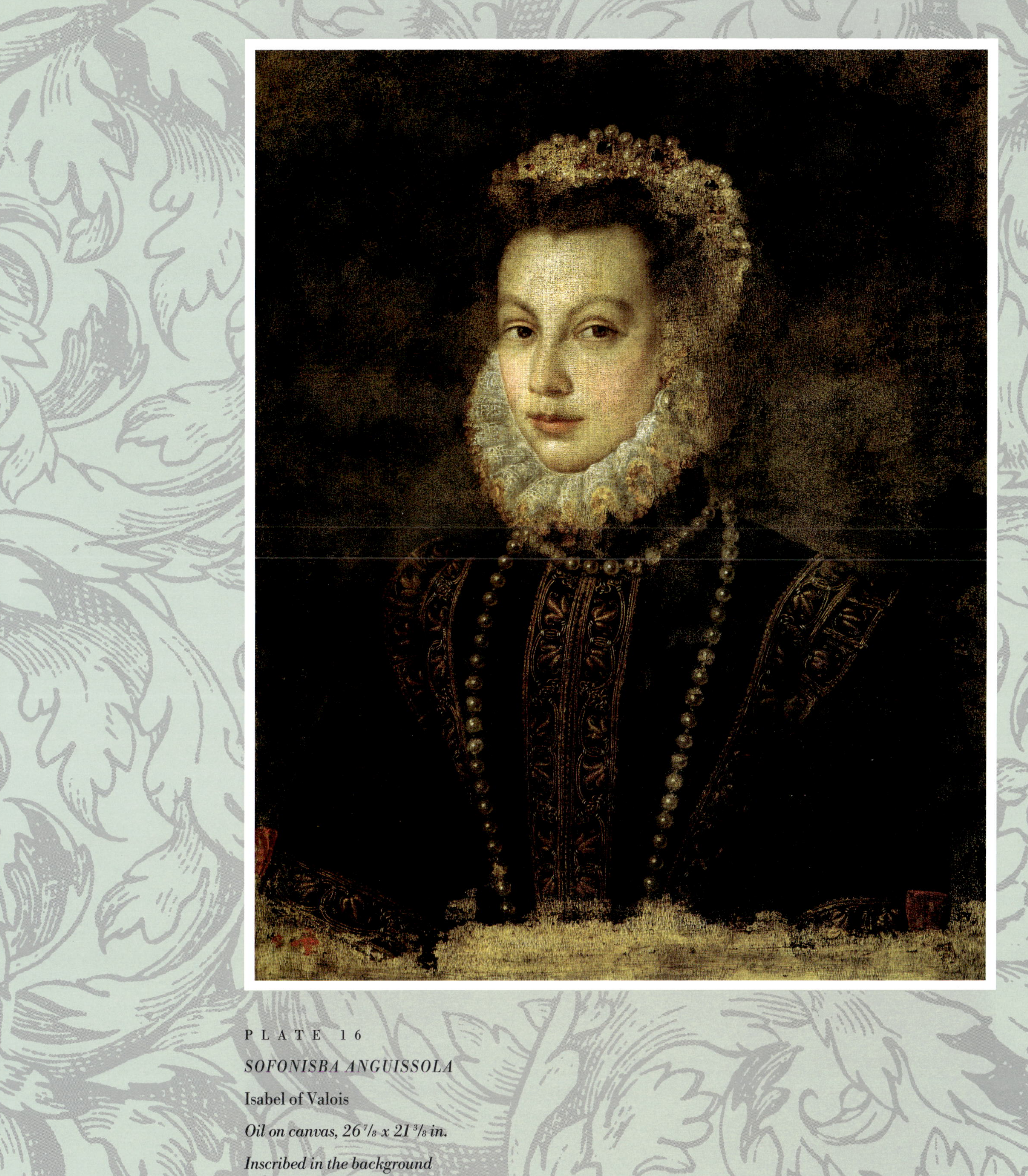

PLATE 16

SOFONISBA ANGUISSOLA

Isabel of Valois

Oil on canvas, 26 7/8 x 21 3/8 in.

Inscribed in the background at left: Sofonisba Lomelina et Anguissola .P.

Vienna, Kunsthistorisches Museum, inv. no. 3351

than anything else, and he is no man of empty promises, he would rather have a sparrow in his hand than a pigeon on the roof.

Diego de Córdoba then adds that, to be able to conclude the matter more quickly and competently, he would like to be sure what exactly the king intended to give whomever would marry her.[62]

Could Ercules Vizconti, of the famous family that was also very influential in Cremona, perhaps have been the suitor of the young Sofonisba who had once been refused by Amilcare? That would explain the brusque reply.

Sofonisba must have been spared these details. After mourning the queen she seems to have looked forward to the forthcoming change in her life with hope and some impatience. An etching by J. N. Muxel of a lost self-portrait (from Passavant, 1851) dates from this period, judging by the collar. This picture indicates that, after so many years in Spain, Sofonisba had incorporated in her attire only the ruffled collar from the Spanish costume. Also, despite this strenuous period of waiting, she had not lost her sense of humor. She presents herself in expensive court garments and bedecked with jewelry, yet wearing a coarse painter's frock over all the splendor. It is as if she wanted to say: despite my respectability and the wealth of presents bestowed on me, I am still, above all, an Italian painter!

During the search for a husband Sofonisba was busy caring for the infantas. They slowly grew old enough for their first lessons in writing and arithmetic. The wait for a husband finally lasted four years. At this time Sofonisba must have transferred all her love for their mother to the little princesses. When they were reunited in Italy after ten and twenty years, they renewed their loving relationship without problems.

A profound change occurred in the life of the palace occupants when Philip II married his niece Anne of Austria in 1570. Her mother, Empress Maria, Philip's sister, had insisted that the duchess of Alba, *Camarera Mayor* and governess of the infantas, should resign her post, since her daughter, the future queen, was able to manage her own affairs. This foreshadowed a much more modest and personal style of running the royal household. The infantas found a loving mother in the unpretentious, modest young woman. A new governess was hired who, together with several of ladies-in-waiting, watched over the well-being of the children. Fourqueveaux, the French ambassador, reported that Sofonisba also minded the infantas while she was still in the country, and Ribera tells that she became their teacher. Sofonisba earned this young queen's affection as well.

Since Sofonisba was not going to remain at court much longer, she was not included on payroll of the new household and no longer received a salary. During her waiting period she had the interest from the queen's bequest at her disposal which, in fact, provided a better living than her previous salary.

When, after a long search and much negotiation, a suitable candidate was finally found for Sofonisba, the king thoughtfully resolved the financial question not with a "reward" for the husband but with a lifelong pension for Sofonisba in the annual amount of 1,000 ducats. He thereby made her financially independent and raised her social position, not that of her husband, in acknowledgment of her services to the royal family. This truly royal compensation for faithful service was also written into the marriage contract, in which the husband assured that he was fully satisfied and would relinquish any claims of a dowry from the parents. Sofonisba must have wanted to protect her family from all eventual claims. The marriage contract, like all marriages in these circles, was drawn up *modo grecorum*, that is, obligating the heirs, in case of the husband's death, to repay the dowry to the widow.[63] Judging Sofonisba's personality from her letters, her vote for or against a candidate must have been considered.

The final decision fell on Don Fabrizio de Moncada. Of Spanish-Italian origin, he was about the same age as Sofonisba. Don Fabrizio was the second son of Francisco de Moncada, who was from one of the most prestigious and aristocratic families in Sicily. His father had once been made Prince of Paternò by Philip II. This meant that Sofonisba would be living at the opposite end of Italy, but all other factors must have seemed highly favorable.

The bridegroom did not travel to Spain for the wedding, probably because his brother had died recently, but was represented by a relative, Don Ferrante de Moncada. On 26 May 1573 the marriage contract was signed by Don Ferrante and Sofonisba. Aside from the pension (to be taken from the taxes of Palermo and Messina) and the dowry, the contract lists the abundant trousseau that the bride brought with her: linens valued at 5,800 scudi, clothes and furniture valued at 3,250 scudi, jewelry and silver valued at 2,785 scudi. The contract contains a separate list with an exact description of the jewelry—expensive presents from the royal couple or other recipients of paintings. All together a value of about 12,000 scudi.

One month later the wedding was celebrated in the chapel of the royal castle, as was customary for ladies-in-waiting. Sofonisba probably wore the white dress embroidered with pearls that Anne of Austria had given her and that, as Ribera could not resist mentioning, was worth 900 scudi. Of this event the indefatigable Maschi writes to the duke of Urbino:

Finally the day of this praiseworthy wedding had come that Sofonisba has so longed for. Don Fabrizio de Moncada, her consort, has sent Don Ferrante from the same house with the authority to finalize it (the wedding). It was carried out accordingly in the presence of the Queen and the noble Princes and Infants, and within the next days she will travel to her husband, with her dowry of more than 20,000 scudi, of which the largest part was given by His Majesty, the King.[64]

The departure would yet be delayed. Philip II in this year wanted to unite the deceased members of the royal family at the Escorial. The coffins of Isabel and Don Carlos would be the first to be transferred, and Sofonisba probably wanted to pay her respects to her queen, Isabel of Valois, one last time before departing. She did not want to miss a repetition of the memorial ceremonies that the king had planned. The mood of the last paintings that Sofonisba made of the royal couple and the infantas, in gratitude and as going-away presents, reflects this somber occasion. She had probably wanted to paint a portrait not only of Queen Anne but also a new one of the king, but had not had thc time because of the preparations for the wedding.

Her *Anne of Austria* (plate 18) adheres to the same concept as the original painting of Philip, but a comparison of both portraits shows what she had learned in the interim. Her technique has become looser, more fluid, her interpretation of the queen's personality more sensitive. With its black dress and the necklace of dark ivory, the portrait is imbued with modesty.

In the *Philip II* (plate 17) the position of the king's right hand matches that of the queen's left. Both are leaning on a chair. The king's left hand is not playing with the fleece of his jacket, as in the original version; rather, the pearls of a rosary run through his fingers. That same year Gregory XIII had introduced the Feast of the Rosary in memory of the victory of faith at the Battle of Lepanto, at which the soldiers of the Armada had prayed with the help of the rosary and pledged their lives to the Virgin. Sofonisba painted a private, intimate version of a theme with symbolic meaning, as she had already done in Italy—the king as defender of the faith. Titian had interpreted that same theme with great pomp, after a suggestion by Philip himself and a sketch by the court painter Sánchez Coello (Madrid, Museo del Prado).

Two small portraits of Sofonisba's students, the *Infanta Isabel Clara Eugenia* (Turin, Galleria Sabauda) and *Infanta Catalina Micaela* (United States, private collection), corresponding to the portraits of the royal couple, must have been painted around the same time. These pictures also must have been changed at the last moment; the children are wearing black necklaces of mourning, evidently for the occasion of the memorial service for the transfer of their mother to the Escorial. However, the black necklaces contrast with the excessively ladylike appearance of Isabel Clara Eugenia and her fashionably plucked eyebrows, not at all childlike nor typical for Sofonisba, and also with the little monkey held by Catalina Micaela.

Sofonisba accompanied Queen Anne to Valsaín in the mountains, where she had fled from the heat in Madrid to wait for the birth of her first child. There Sofonisba must have received the news of her father's death in early July, just when, after her long absence abroad, she had hoped finally to see him again within the next few weeks. On 3 July a document, drawn up by the notary in Segovia, was sent to her brother in Cremona. According to the document, he would receive her lifetime pension from that point on.

The news of her father's death must have made Sofonisba's desire to travel home as quickly as possible even more urgent. The news of the death of Infanta Juana, who had been a center of calm at the court during all of Sofonisba's years in Spain, and a source of strength for everyone, must have reached her en route, or perhaps once she arrived in Palermo. Both deaths overshadowed the long-awaited return to Italy.

Sofonisba's Return to Italy: The Years in Sicily[65]

We do not know if Sofonisba traveled to Cremona to see her mother and siblings after her fourteen-year absence and to share their grief before her arrival in Palermo. She must have had a choice between taking the more direct route of Valencia-Balearic Isles-Sicily or the longer, but safer, one of Barcelona-Genoa-Sicily, which avoided the danger of pirate attacks. This would have been a unique opportunity to go to Cremona within a few days. Perhaps the visit with her family during their time of mourning was so brief and so discreet that not even the town chronicler, Antonio Campi, was alerted. We do know that Sofonisba arrived in Palermo before 2 October. A document of that date exists, signed by both spouses, in which Don Fabrizio bequeaths the inventory of his house to Sofonisba, in the case of his death, in return perhaps for everything that she brought into the marriage.[66]

Sofonisba and Don Fabrizio's marriage must have been harmonious during its brief span of only five years, as the tone of this document already intimates. Sofonisba brought glamour to Don Fabrizio's life, which had been dominated by his older, first-born brother, Cesare. The ambiance that surrounded her as lady-in-waiting, favored by the monarch, and her fame as a painter made her intriguing to the members of the Sicilian court and to society on the island. Ribera writes that she continued to maintain her connections to the Spanish court and received further proof of goodwill:

Therefore she was popular with the viceroy and all royal officials and was able to return many favors herself on formal and other occasions; and because this lady so loved her art, she did not hesitate to practice it, and painted not only portraits but also many religious works of such excellence that no one equaled her in that profession.[67]

This account describes the agreeable aspects of Sofonisba's life. The dissatisfactory ones, which also must have become public knowledge, were ignored by the chronicler. Not only did an epidemic of the plague break out at the time, which ravaged Sicily, especially her husband's town of Paternò, but Sofonisba also became entangled in a family drama that made her an impoverished widow after five years of marriage.

Fabrizio, as the second-born son, was dependent on his older brother, Cesare de Moncada, the Prince of Paternò. After his brother's death in 1572, Fabrizio became dependent on his sister-in-law, Luisa de Luna, a member of a prominent Spanish family and the mother of his brother's only male heir. Sofonisba and her husband spent a large part of the year in his brother's palace in Paternò, while the prince's family resided in Palermo. As the *governatore* of Paternò, Fabrizio received only an annual stipend of 400 ducats. Sofonisba's pension and dowry were, therefore, a very welcome source of income to Don Fabrizio. Nevertheless, the combined income seems to have been insufficient for their life spent partly in Paternò, at that time a somewhat important town, and partly in Palermo, where they participated in social occasions at the viceroyal court. In 1574, only one year after the wedding, Sofonisba was forced to pawn one of her expensive diamond rings as security for a loan. Shortly thereafter, 800 ducats out of Sofonisba's pension of 1,000 ducats were distributed to support the military forces in Paternò. Only one-fifth of Sofonisba's funds remained at the couple's disposal.

Just as Fabrizio was dependent for his income on his sister-in-law Luisa, the guardian of her son, Francesco, so would her husband's oldest brother, her brother-in-law Fabrizio, become her son's legal custodian if she remarried. In that case, she would be dependent on him. The relationship between Luisa and Fabrizio must have been strained by this mutual dependency. When Luisa planned her remarriage to Antonio de

PLATE • 17

Philip II, the son of Emperor Charles V and Isabel of Portugal born in 1527 in Valladolid, became king of Spain in 1556, when his father abdicated the throne. Under his rule Spain achieved full hegemony among the European powers, for which Charles V had paved the way and which led to Spain's massive intervention in the politics of Italy, France and the Holy Roman Empire. Spain's role was not perceptibly diminished by setbacks, such as the defection of the Netherlands or the defeat of the Spanish Armada against England. Philip's certainty of his country's leadership position made it possible for him to insist on the enforcement of the Catholic faith and prompted his zealous intolerance of confessional issues. His four marriages—with Maria of Portugal in 1543; Mary Tudor, queen of England, in 1554; Isabel of Valois in 1559; and Anne of Austria in 1570—were politically motivated. Philip's interest in the arts was expressed by generous patronage, through commissions for Italian, Netherlandish, and Spanish artists and his own passionate collecting. Philip died in 1598 at the Escorial, the monastic residence that he had built, a widower since 1580.

A bust-length portrait, this picture is personal in character and differs from official portraits. Its miniaturist details remind one more of Italian examples than do Sofonisba's other paintings from her time in Spain. Although this painting, like most of the other Spanish portraits by Sofonisba, had been attributed to Alonso Sánchez Coello, Angulo suspected that Sofonisba Anguissola might be the author (exh. cat. Madrid 1963, 612). A comparison with Sofonisba's other works (Kusche 1989, 409), as well as the results of technical examinations (Garrido in exh. cat. Madrid 1990, 227), confirm this attribution.

X-rays show that the severe black coat of the king originally had a different shape and probably a different color. The king held his right hand to his chest. In its current form, as a pendant to *Anne of Austria*, probably 1573 (plate 18), the king's portrait certainly was not created at the same time (Breuer 1984, 87; exh. cat. Madrid 1990, no. 10: c. 1575), but much earlier, perhaps around 1565. This date is suggested partly by the fact that his face is still youthful and his expression content.

Exh. cat. Cremona 1994, 99, 104, 134, no. 26 (M. Kusche)

—*KARL SCHÜTZ*

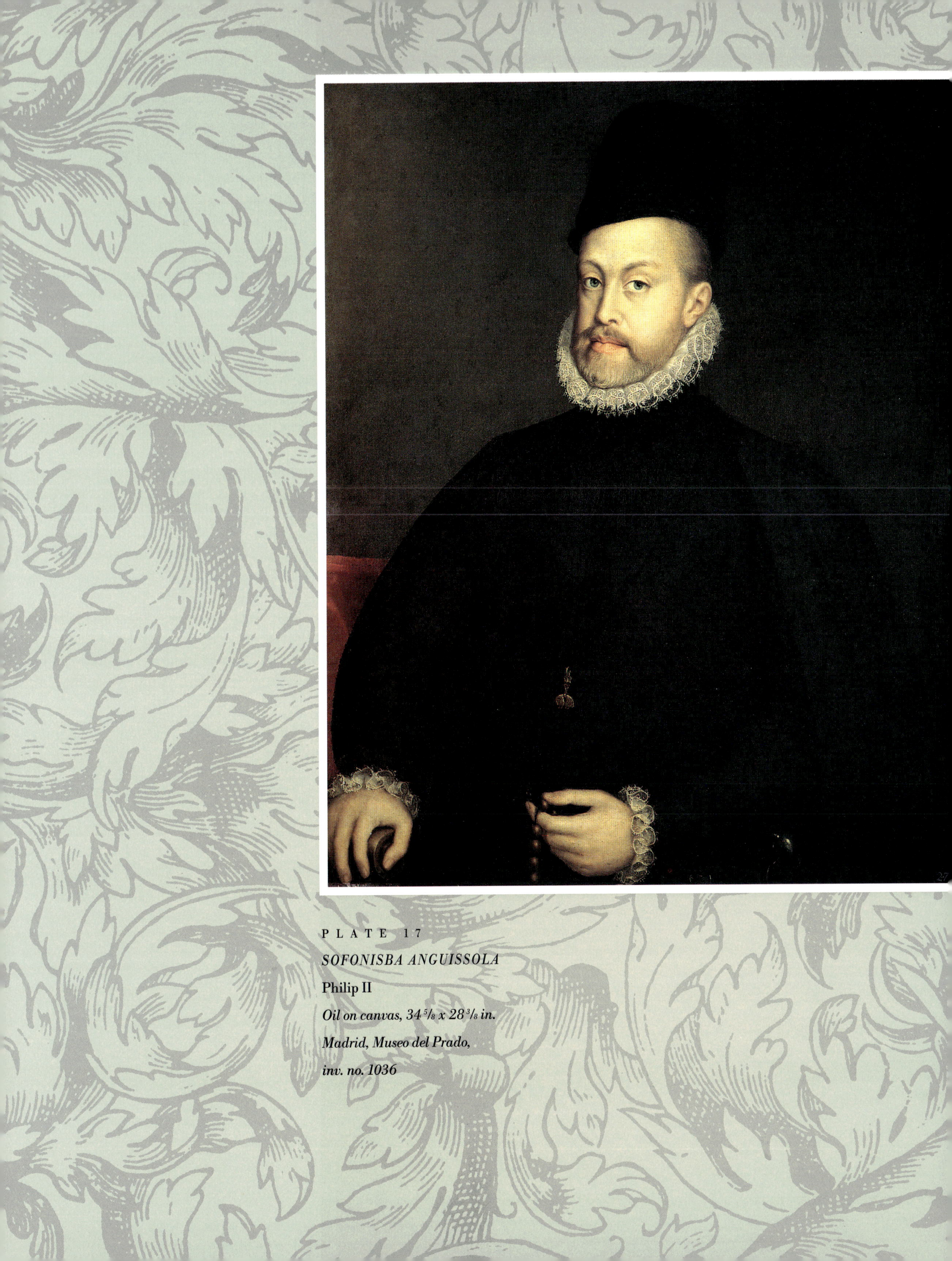

PLATE 17

SOFONISBA ANGUISSOLA

Philip II

Oil on canvas, 34 5/8 x 28 3/8 in.

Madrid, Museo del Prado,

inv. no. 1036

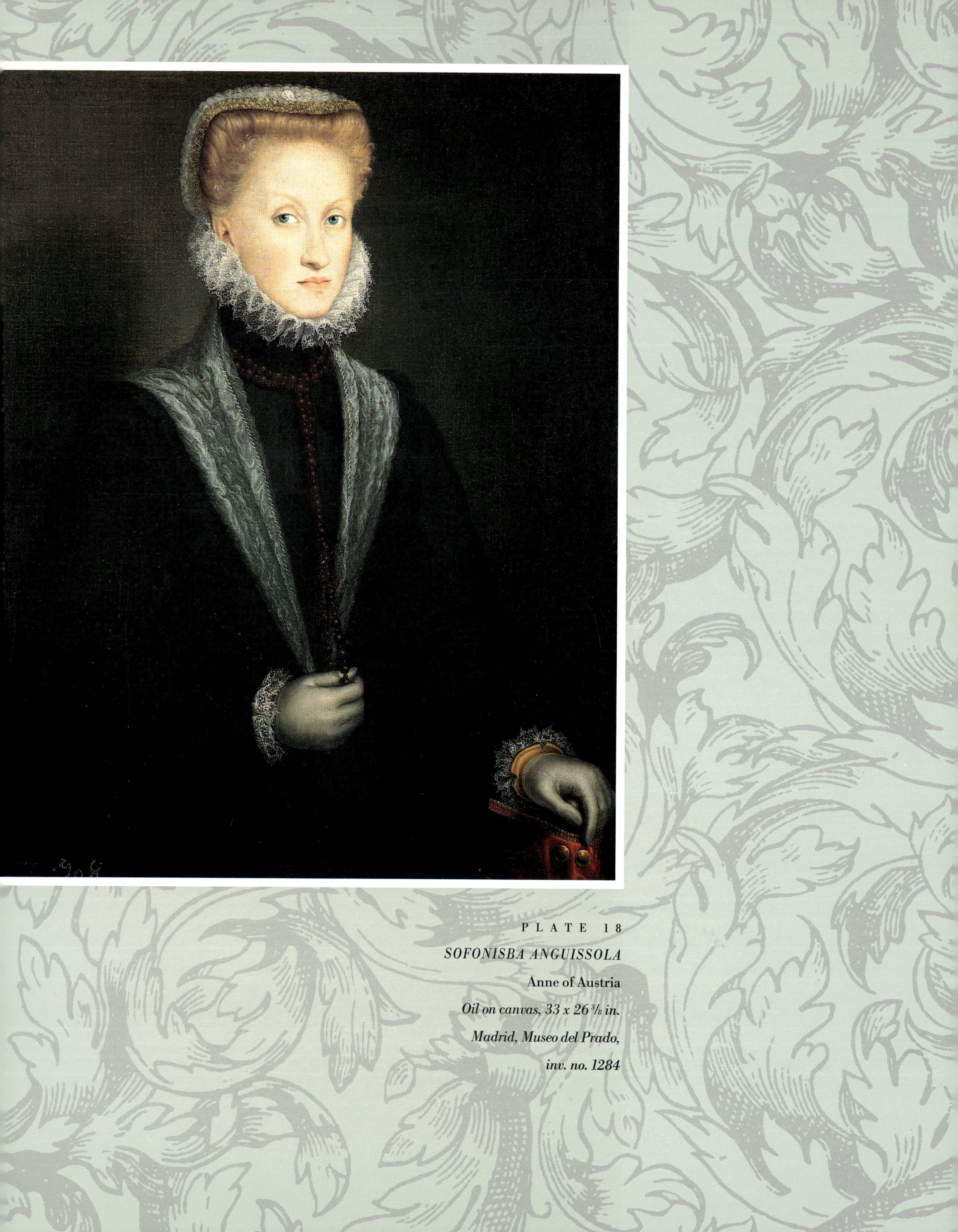

PLATE 18

SOFONISBA ANGUISSOLA

Anne of Austria

Oil on canvas, 33 x 26 3/8 in.

Madrid, Museo del Prado,

inv. no. 1284

PLATE • 18

Anne, the oldest daughter of Maximilian II and the Infanta Maria, was born in 1549 in Cigales, Spain. Originally chosen as the wife of Don Carlos, after his death she married Philip II, her uncle, on 12 November 1570. She was his fourth wife. Over the course of her ten-year marriage she had six children, of whom only the Infante Philip, who would later become king and the successor to Philip II, would survive. Queen Anne died of the flu on October 26, 1580, on her way to Portugal. Philip II had claimed the Portuguese crown after the death of his nephew, King Sebastian.

The bust-length size of this portrait of Queen Anne indicates that it was intended to be more personal than official in character. The simple elegance of the queen's clothing reflects the religious tenets of the Spanish court. Not least for this characteristic, the portrait long has been seen as a pendant to *Philip II* (plate 17) a work of almost equal size. It originally was not attributed to Sofonisba but to an unknown collaborator or follower of the court painter Alonso Sánchez Coello (cat. Madrid 1963, 617). Both works are by the same hand, however (Kusche 1964, 194), as ascertained by further investigation (Kusche 1989, 414). Technical examination bears out this attribution because of coinciding characteristics in the painting technique (exh. cat. Madrid 1990, no. 9; Garrido, exh. cat. Madrid 1990, 226).

Nevertheless, differences exist between the painting of the king and its counterpart, the portrait of Anne, manifested in the more relaxed and deft, yet delicate and precise execution. The rendering resembles that of the much later *Infanta Catalina Micaela* (plate 19). Thus an earlier date suggests itself for the Philip II than for that of the queen, which may have been painted in 1573, the last year of Sofonisba's residence in Spain.

Contrary to the *Anne of Austria* by Alonso Sánchez Coello (Vienna, Kunsthistorisches Museum), which adheres to the rules for Spanish court portraiture, Sofonisba's portrait concentrates on the half-figure and is, thereby, much more immediate and intimate. It reflects her perceptive grasp of her subject's personality. Capturing her models' human and individual side was a paramount concern for the artist.

Exh. cat. Cremona 1994, 104, 135, no. 27 (M. Kusche)

—*KARL SCHÜTZ*

Aragón in 1577, a member of one of the most important Spanish-Italian families, the engaged couple decided to marry their underage children to one another to avoid any interference in their affairs. That aggravated the conflict. Fabrizio justly feared that Antonio de Aragón, in his dual role as stepfather and father-in-law of Francesco, would try to take over the custodianship of the boy, with the support of the Luna and Aragón families, who had influence at the court. He saw this as a threat to his own position in Paternò and a threat to the inheritance of his nephew Francesco, which might someday become his own inheritance as the second in succession to the Moncada estate. In a memorandum to the king he openly voiced his concern. When the king did not react quickly enough and the two marriages took place, the Moncada-Anguissola couple needed to act urgently so they would not be crushed by the Luna-Aragón alliance. Sofonisba must have been convinced that a direct audience with the king would help them attain justice. Without taking the time to leave a will, which was customary before such a journey, Fabrizio seized the first opportunity. He departed for Spain on 25 April 1578 on a galley belonging to the duke of Terranova, Don Carlos de Aragón y Taviglia, one of the foremost military leaders of the day and a diplomat in the service of Philip II.

Between Palermo and Naples, at the latitude of Capri, the galley was captured by pirates and Fabrizio de Moncada drowned. He was the only one of the noblemen who did not make it to shore. The reaction to Don Fabrizio's death is curiously weak. Philip II learned of the galley's loss only two months later, in a letter from the viceroy of Naples, the Marqués de Mondéjar. The letter, which is mainly intended to convey the duke of Terranova's request for forgiveness regarding the loss of the ship, does not even mention Don Fabrizio's death. Only in the enclosed memorandum,[68] which gives a very dramatic account of the chase of the galley by the pirates, is Don Fabrizio's death casually mentioned: "He was the only one who drowned." There is no word of regret or any other comment, while the conduct of the duke de Terranova is described in detail and with approbation.

The fact that the duke of Terranova, who was an Aragón, neglected to tell the viceroy of Naples of Don Fabrizio's death certainly must be due to Terranova's dislike of the deceased. One could pursue the matter further and assume that not much of an effort was made to rescue him—Fabrizio's death, after all, saved the Aragón family from the king's intervention in the matter of the custodianship and, thereby, in the matter of the Moncada inheritance.

Hard times began for Sofonisba. In addition to the loss of her husband, she now was completely dependent on a family set against her. Now the provision in the marriage contract should have gone into effect, according to which her dowry would be returned by the family, including the jewelry pawned by Don Fabrizio. But the family was unwilling to pay even the smallest sum. Sofonisba was forced to file a lawsuit, which would remain unresolved for over fifteen years, until, finally, justice was granted. An added dilemma was that

Fabrizio had withdrawn not only the rent for the current year but also the one for 1579, to cover the costs of the journey.

Sofonisba must soon have related these events to the royal family. The reaction was immediate: the king wanted her to come back. But Sofonisba, writes the chronicler Ribera, "had already served for many years" and she must have wanted to be with her aging mother in Cremona. The death of her sister in January of this disastrous year must have been a contributing factor in this decision. Aside from her mother, only her brother, Asdrubale, and her sister Anna Maria still lived in Cremona. Asdrubale arrived in October or November 1578 to help her resolve the financial problems in Palermo and dissolve her household. The move was again delayed, however. Sofonisba probably still was hoping for a solution to her financial distress from the Moncadas or the king. But the court also had experienced a difficult year in 1578. Three members of the family had died–the king's nephews–the Archduke Wenzel and King Sebastian of Portugal–and, finally, his successor, Fernando. Sofonisba's troubles must not have received much attention while the royal family had so many of their own.

Over a year after her brother's arrival, in December 1579, Sofonisba and Asdrubale finally boarded a galley bound for Genoa with the household. Sofonisba left the hardest years of her life behind. Her artistic career also was affected by the adverse circumstances of that time. No works of art are known from those years. From a later source it can be assumed that she mainly painted miniatures in Sicily. Contact with other painters must have been scarce, and the level of artistic accomplishment on the island was modest.

Marriage to Orazio Lomellini in Pisa[69]

On 17 December 1579 the siblings arrived on the Genoese ship in Livorno, located near Pisa in the duchy of Tuscany. Over the course of the voyage, Sofonisba's life took a dramatic turn: she decided to get married again. On the trip, or perhaps even just before the departure from Palermo, she had met the Genoese captain of the ship, Orazio Lomellini, who regularly navigated the route from Genoa to Palermo and back. Palermo had a large colony of Genoese merchants, who traded with Spain and the Orient and used Lomellini's shipping service as their link to Genoa. It must have been love at first sight; both made their decision very quickly. The chronicler means to be gallant when he attributes the decision to Orazio's insistence: "On the journey that nobleman so politely pursued her that she had no choice but to promise him that she would be his wife."[70]

That Sofonisba very much wished for this marriage to take place, and soon, can be concluded from the fact that she made her decision against her brother's wishes and without asking the king's permission. She probably wanted to avoid the endless bureaucracy and the waiting period that an inquiry from the king would entail, as she had learned from recent experience. Perhaps she was not sure that the king would be pleased with Orazio Lomellini–he was descended from one of the important Genoese families but born out of wedlock, although officially recognized, and had no fortune or social rank.

We learn this detail and others in a riveting exchange of correspondence between Sofonisba and Francesco de' Medici, duke of Tuscany, which again gives us an opportunity to admire her style and intelligence. In a letter from Pisa on 18 December 1579 she asks the duke to forgive the customs for her household goods and reminds him of their acquaintance in Spain. She mentions neither her intent to marry nor the presence of her brother, much less that of Orazio Lomellini, but only lets the duke know that she is lodging at the Convent of San Matteo.

The duke responds on 24 December. He never broaches the customs issue but immediately addresses her marriage plans. His network of informants must have been outstanding. Francesco de' Medici reminds Sofonisba to weigh this step carefully—her decision seems unwise to him. His interest shows how highly he regarded Sofonisba. But the letter probably was not prompted just by his feeling for her. He also must have been concerned that, on his soil, no decision should be made of which the king would not approve by someone who had been in such close personal service to the king. At the very least Francesco wished to protect himself by warning her:

As I have heard that Your Honor is currently in Pisa, with the intention to marry—against the wishes of your family and below the rank of your house—I wish to remind you to reconsider this issue, since I am acquainted with you from the time at the court of the Spanish king and because of the affection I have always felt for you as the servant of Your Majesty. You should not only inform him about your intentions but you should also choose a subject that is suitable for you, your house, and your service to such a noble master. Feelings often dictate a path that seems useful and honorable at the time, but which later, tempered by reason, turns out to be the complete opposite, and then regret is often in vain. But I am convinced that you will do the right thing, as the intelligent woman for which I have always taken you, and I am sure that you do not wish to lose the good name that you have acquired through much labor. I am available for anything you deem advisable and useful. May God grant you every certainty.[71]

Sofonisba countered the Duke's note with a very witty and also very diplomatic one of her own, which reveals her confident personality, well-versed in court games:

I received a letter from Your Serene Highness that comforted me in my struggles, as I saw with how much benevolence Your Highness remembers me in a matter so important to me and cautions me of my duties. I assure Your Highness that even if Your Highness had not illustrated all the obligations that Your Highness mentions, it would have been sufficient for me to know that I—not only in this matter, about which Your Highness was given erroneous information, but also in any conceivable other, which would be much to my advantage—had not acted according to Your Highness' wishes, to put my own conviction second to what Your Highness would recommend I do. But since marriages are made in heaven and not on earth, Your Highness' letter reached me too late, so that I am unable to prove Your Highness my loyal servitude. I beg Your Highness as much as I can to forgive me and extend your goodwill toward me in the future, and to continue to count me among your loyal servants. With that in mind I beg Our Lord that he may grant Your Serene person the greatest conceivable good fortune.[72]

It follows from this charming letter, which tells the duke about the fait accompli and which is not without gentle irony and avoids any justification, that she was already married on 24 December. Perhaps she married on that day, hastily, in reaction to the letter, to preempt any interference or because Christmas Eve seemed like a day of blessing for the beginning of a marriage. After all, this marriage was one after her own heart, with which for the first time she had made a decision about her life completely in accordance with her own wishes.

Her instincts proved excellent. The marriage was truly to her advantage. The happiness of the union lasted a lifetime, and the spouses were universally respected. The duke was the first to concur. After closer inquiries, and on Sofonisba's written request, he received Orazio Lomellini graciously and favorably. The king, too, informed by Sofonisba about the event, finally gave his *placet*. Asdrubale, the brother who had been against the marriage since he probably had counted on Sofonisba, as a widow, to settle in Cremona and provide financial support and company for their mother, was persuaded as well. He soon visited Sofonisba and Orazio in Genoa.

While the couple was still in Pisa, the first distribution from the pension in Palermo arrived on 2 March 1580, through Sofonisba's representative in Milan. On 17 March a new contract was drawn up in Pisa for the dowry. Sofonisba's share was to be the same amount as in the first dowry for Don Fabrizio. But she and Orazio would have to wait many more years to recover the capital of 6,000 scudi from the Moncadas. The pension, her second source of revenue, however, was collected by Orazio, as her representative, from May 1581.

Did the belated blessing of the king reach them there in Pisa or in Genoa, or was his message postponed due to another death? Queen Anne died of a bout of flu late in 1580, on her way to Portugal, where the king had gone to assume the inherited succession to the Portuguese throne. Her loss affected the king severely, and it must also have caused Sofonisba great sadness. In the course of 1580 the couple left Pisa. The exact date is not known.

The Genoa Years[73]

The married couple of Lomellini resided in Genoa at the latest from early 1581 on. Around that time the Empress Maria, Philip II's sister, returned to Spain after the death of her husband, Maximilian II, to spend the remainder of her life there, as other family members had done. She stopped in Genoa. On the way, she received the news of the unexpected death of her daughter Anne. Sofonisba went to call on her, and must have been able to console her with her memories of the queen. She gave the empress a small painting of the Madonna, and may have painted her portrait.

The acquaintance with the empress turned out to be beneficial for Sofonisba. Without doubt she used the opportunity to introduce her husband and to ask for the noble lady's support with the king. After a visit with Philip II in Lisbon, Sofonisba finally—by now it was January 1583—received a sum of 500 ducats "as assistance on the occasion of the death of Fabrizio Moncada." This was five years after his death! The payment, long authorized by the king, had been held back, perhaps, at first, due to the chronic lack of funds. More delay may have been caused by Sofonisba's new circumstances, or the changes in the royal household.

After the king's belated consent to her marriage, either Sofonisba or Orazio asked Philip II for help. We do not know exactly what they requested, but it was most likely a financial contribution, a position with an income or a rank for Orazio. This is evident from her letter of 14 October 1583, the only

P L A T E • 1 9

The Infanta Catalina Micaela, the second daughter of Philip II and Isabel of Valois, was born on 10 October 1567. In 1585 she married to Duke Charles Emanuel of Savoy. She died in Turin on November 6, 1597, giving birth to her tenth child. At her court the Italian, Spanish and French culture coalesced in felicitous accord.

This painting was attributed to Alonso Sánchez Coello until recently, and thought to be one of his most important works (exh. cat. Madrid 1990, no. 28). Allende-Salazar, however, considered it to be by an Italian artist, based on the painting technique (exh. cat. Madrid 1963, 614). This assumption was confirmed by technical examination of the work (Garrido in exh. cat. Madrid 1990, 224). The attribution to Sofonisba (Kusche 1989, 415) is based first on the unusually liberated brushwork that is characteristic of her but not of Sánchez Coello, as well as on the discovery of a document (exh. cat. Cremona 1994, 388), which makes a meeting with Sofonisba very probable on the infanta's trip to Turin in 1585. Sofonisba lived in Genoa at that time. Sofonisba's husband, Orazio Lomellini, was captain of a ship that took a Genoese delegation to Savona to greet the infanta, who had interrupted her travels for a visit. Sofonisba seems to have participated in the welcoming ceremony, because the poet Gabriello Chiabrera of Savona later regretted in a letter that he had not been able to see Sofonisba while she was visiting his hometown.

Exh. cat. Cremona 1994, 111, 140, no. 30 (M. Kusche)

—*KARL SCHÜTZ*

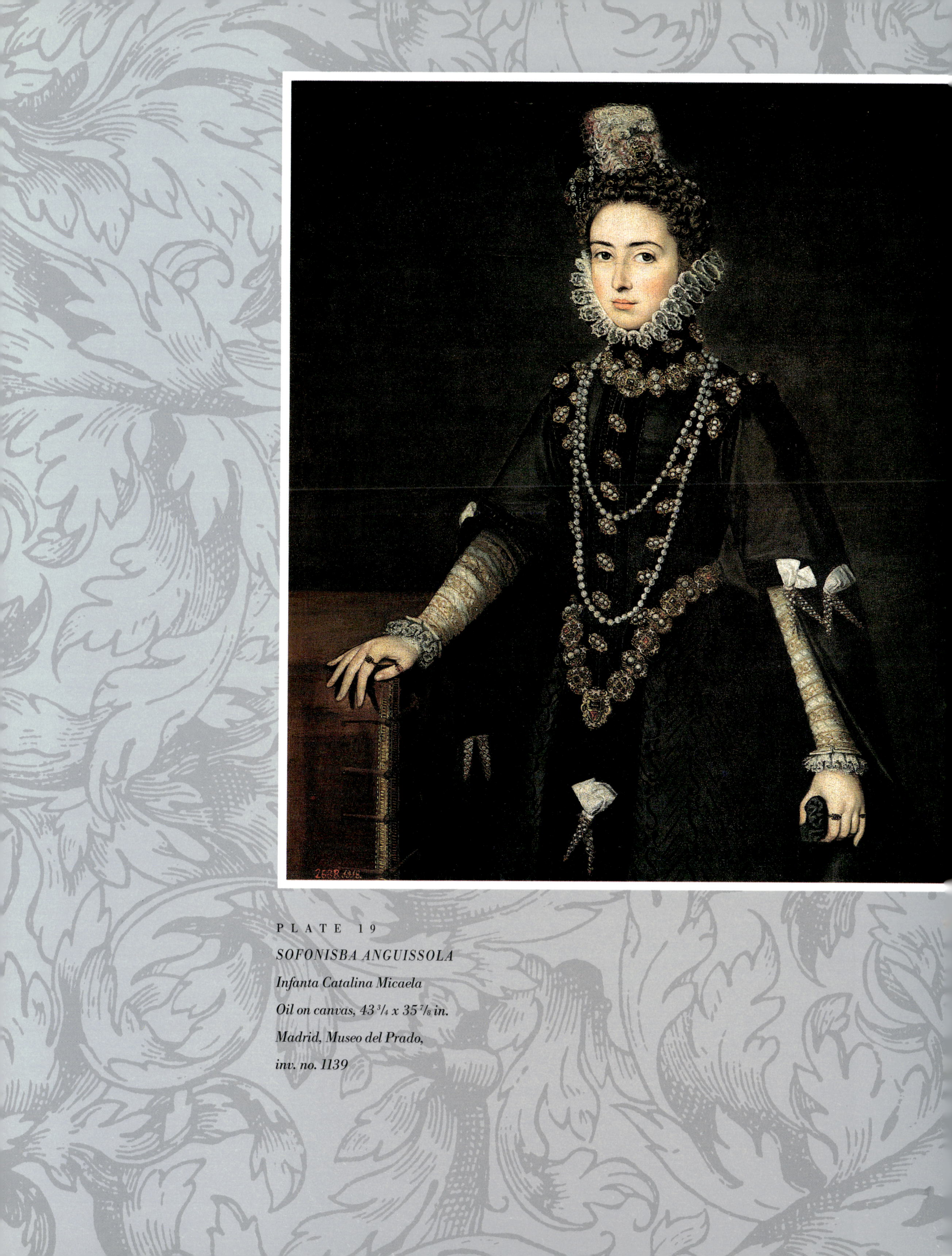

PLATE 19

SOFONISBA ANGUISSOLA

Infanta Catalina Micaela

Oil on canvas, 43 ¾ x 35 ⅞ in.

Madrid, Museo del Prado,

inv. no. 1139

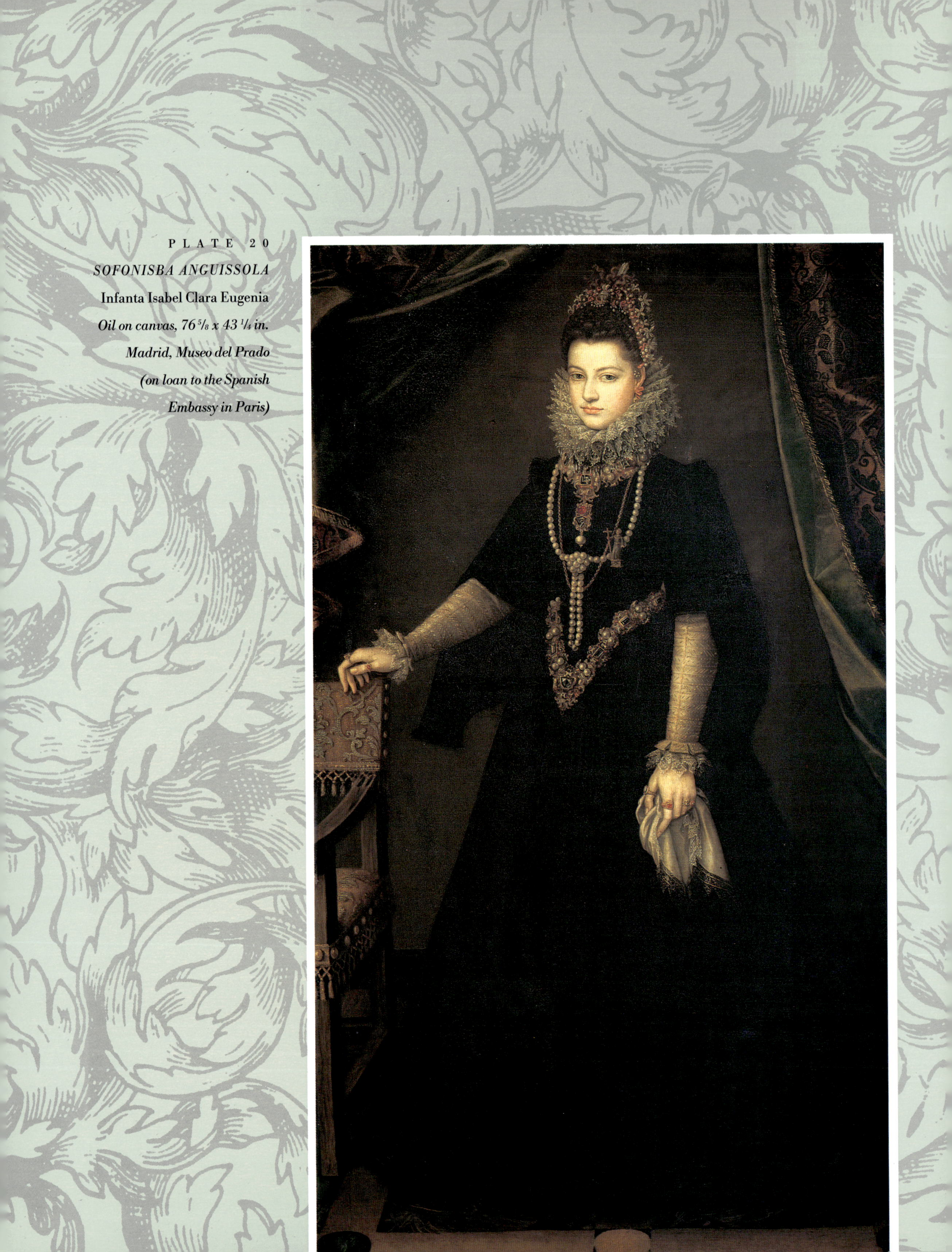

PLATE 20

SOFONISBA ANGUISSOLA

Infanta Isabel Clara Eugenia

Oil on canvas, 76 5/8 x 43 1/4 in.

Madrid, Museo del Prado (on loan to the Spanish Embassy in Paris)

In his biography of Sofonisba Anguissola (see exh. cat. Cremona 1994, 409-11), published in 1609, Pietro Paolo de Ribera was the first to mention that the artist had painted a life-size portrait of the Infanta Isabel Clara Eugenia, when the Infanta briefly stopped in Genoa on her way to the Netherlands in 1599. She had just been married and was accompanied by her husband, the Archduke Albert. De Ribera reports further that the painting could not be completed within the short period of time available, probably because of its large format as an official state portrait.

Although the existence of the portrait was long known from this source, it was thought to be lost until recently, when it was identified as the portrait shown here (Kusche 1992b, 25). This portrait of the infanta, painted in Genoa, had neither been sent to Brussels, as de Ribera believed, nor to Vienna, but instead went to Spain. It is mentioned for the first time in the inventory of the Alcázar, which was compiled after the death of Philip II, together with the three-quarter-length *Isabel of Valois* (compare plate 14). The name of the artist is not given for either painting, but the portrait is immediately recognizable by one specific detail mentioned in the inventory—the small statue of Saint Anthony of Padua, which the infanta wears on a golden chain around her neck.

Exh. cat. Cremona 1994, 113, 147, no. 31 (M. Kusche)

—*KARL SCHÜTZ*

PLATE • 20

one to the king that is known, in which flashes of Sofonisba's personality sparkle between the formal wording:

I have written to Your Majesty together with Orazio, my husband, and have asked Your Majesty to honor me by recommending his wish to Your Majesty, not only on his own behalf but also for him as my husband. Again I am turning to Your Majesty to favor me in the aforementioned affair and in the hope that, since it is a common favor, it will be granted very shortly. In my trust in the well-known benevolence and generosity which Your Majesty shows Your Majesty's servants, among whom I count myself as Your Majesty's most loyal one, it cannot fail that a good outcome will be granted, as I cannot expect any differently from the royal hands of Your Majesty, on which after God my entire future welfare depends. I will add this debt of gratitude to the many others I owe Your Majesty, whose hands I kiss with every possible demonstration of reverence and humility. Asking Our Lord to keep the Catholic royal person of Your Majesty alive for many and the happiest years.[74]

The king reacted relatively quickly. In June 1584 Sofonisba's pension from Palermo was increased from the original 1,000 ducats by another one of 300 ducats. The king again, as he had done with the first marriage, did not give the amount to the husband but to Sofonisba, so that "she would be able to add this debt of gratitude to the many others," directly, without a circuitous route by way of her husband.

In Genoa, Sofonisba enjoyed the satisfaction of being cordially received by her husband's family, evidently from the beginning, as is apparent from a number of portraits that she painted for the Lomellini. With marriage and family circumstances now happily resolved, a time of artistic and social blossoming began for Sofonisba. She was no longer the young girl who enchanted her observers with her poise and liveliness, but had become a great lady. This fact is corroborated by the contemporary opinion of an important man, the master of ceremonies for the republic of Genoa, Pater Gerolamo Bordoni. He was impressed with Sofonisba not only as an artist, a *virtuosa*, but also as a personality: *ornata d'una gravità signorile, e d'una certa affabile grandezza*.

Artists and literati were frequent visitors at the house. Sofonisba must have met Luca Cambiaso before he left for Spain in 1583 with a troupe of painting assistants, to help with the fresco painting in the Escorial. Sofonisba admired his ingratiating art very much. Many years after his departure she still copied from his paintings, as in 1588 with the *Nursing Madonna*, today in Budapest (plate 23), and again in 1592 with *The Holy Family with Saints Anne and John the Baptist* (plate 24).

Sofonisba must have followed with great interest the work of many of Philip II's Italian painters of that generation, frequently hired for the embellishment of the Escorial. In 1585 Federigo Zuccaro left with a baggage train of assistants and supplies, and in 1588 Pellegrino Tibaldi went. The recurrent travels of these and other artists, who boarded ship in Genoa and later returned there, also meant contact with the court and the opportunity to send and receive mail.

Sofonisba established a close relationship with the Castello family of painters in Genoa. Her ties to this Genoese dynasty of painters must have stemmed from her time in Spain when Giovanni Battista Castello, called "il Bergamasco," worked, first with a group of Genoese and later with his sons, as architect, painter and sculptor on the decoration of the Alcázar and of the country estates El Pardo and Valsaín. In Genoa, Sofonisba was especially close to Bernardo Castello and his brother Giovanni Battista, "il Genovese." She also was the godmother of one of each of their sons. Since the latter was an excellent miniaturist, her interest in miniature painting may have provided the connection.

Aside from those smaller works and the religious paintings after Cambiaso (plates 23 and 24), many portraits, especially of family and friends, were painted, some in larger format, as old inventories show. In Genoa she also resumed teaching, which she had enjoyed with her sisters and Queen Isabel. She seems to have devoted some of her time to training Pietro Francesco Piola as a miniaturist. Sofonisba would not have had a male pupil of high rank—her repertoire was too limited—but she did pass on her enthusiasm and, perhaps, her abilities to other women. The remark by the Cremonese chronicler Antonio Campi about her time in Genoa, in which the ladies of the period are mentioned, may be interpreted as support for this assumption: "She now lives in that excellent town, most revered by all, and with the best reputation, and she is not only very famous but also much admired by all the consequential noble ladies of that town for her art."[75] Even after the turn of the century, during her last years in Cremona, when her eyesight finally began to fail, she is said to have taken pleasure in giving artistic advice.

Although not one of the many portraits she painted of her family and friends in Genoa has been found to date, some of her official works have survived from that long mature period of her life—from 1580/81 until the second decade of the 17th century. Only representations of personalities at the Spanish court from this period have survived, as they were well protected because of their importance for dynastic and historical reasons. The full range of Sofonisba's artistic potential is apparent in these portraits.

The only signed portrait of these is the previously mentioned replica after her first *Isabel of Valois*, which is signed *Sofonisba Lomelina Anguissola P.* (plate 16). Although it is not in good condition, it demonstrates how the painter's technique has changed since her stay in Spain. The features of the queen are treated very delicately, now completely after Correggio; the ruffled collar seems foamy, the shadows as though applied with a quick breath. The incipient talent seen in her Spanish works is now fully realized.

Further royal portraits were painted in this period because Sofonisba could not have chosen any better location in Italy than Genoa in which to cultivate her Spanish contacts. Genoa was the crossroads, not just for connecting northern and southern Italian estates or spheres of power. Since land travel through France was not possible, Genoa was also the point of departure for the land route to the Netherlands.

The year 1585 brought an event that must have moved Sofonisba deeply. The Infanta Catalina Micaela, her student as a child, married the duke of Savoy. A Genoese delegation was sent to greet her on her way to her husband's estate of Turin, with a welcoming ceremony in the Genoese city of Savona. Orazio Lomellini, the captain of the

PLATE • 21

A painting which could also be called the "flight to Egypt" for its imagery, this work came to the Accademia Carrara in Bergamo from the collection of the famous connoisseur and art historian Giovanni Morelli.

The composition of nearly all religious paintings by Sofonisba or her sisters is based on existing works by other artists. The well-known letter by their father, Amilcare Anguissola, to Michelangelo is a case in point, wherein he asks Michelangelo for one of his drawings so his daughter could render it in oil *(perché lei lo colorisse in olio).*

Artists from Lombardy in particular were trained to work from nature, and to use the *disegno,* the invention, of other artists for narrative paintings. This Lombard realism, the work *dal naturale,* was considered a deficiency in teaching, of which the Lombard painter Michelangelo Caravaggio later was accused (compare also Gregori in exh. cat. Cremona 1994, 16).

In this case Sofonisba's work is based on a composition by Camillo Boccaccino, who was stylistically close to Francesco Mazzola Parmigianino. The original composition is still extant as a painting in the Art Gallery in Glasgow and as a drawing in the Pinacoteca Ambrosiana in Milan (di Giampaolo 1978, 82; Sambo in exh. cat. Cremona 1985, 176). Both works can be dated to the second half of the 1530s. Compared to its original, the painting by Sofonisba appears less painterly, more precisely executed and denser in its plasticity. Only the landscape in the background seems more influenced by the atmospheric tonality of the original work, which she presents with an outright Venetian openness, usually foreign to her.

The stylistic discrepancies between Sofonisba's own narrative paintings have sometimes confused the research on her, since the variety of prototypes was not sufficiently considered.

Two further versions of the composition are known, one of them signed, in which other saints are added (exh. cat. Cremona 1994, 35, fig. 6).

Exh. cat. Cremona 1994, no. 33 (V. Guazzoni)

—*WOLFGANG PROHASKA*

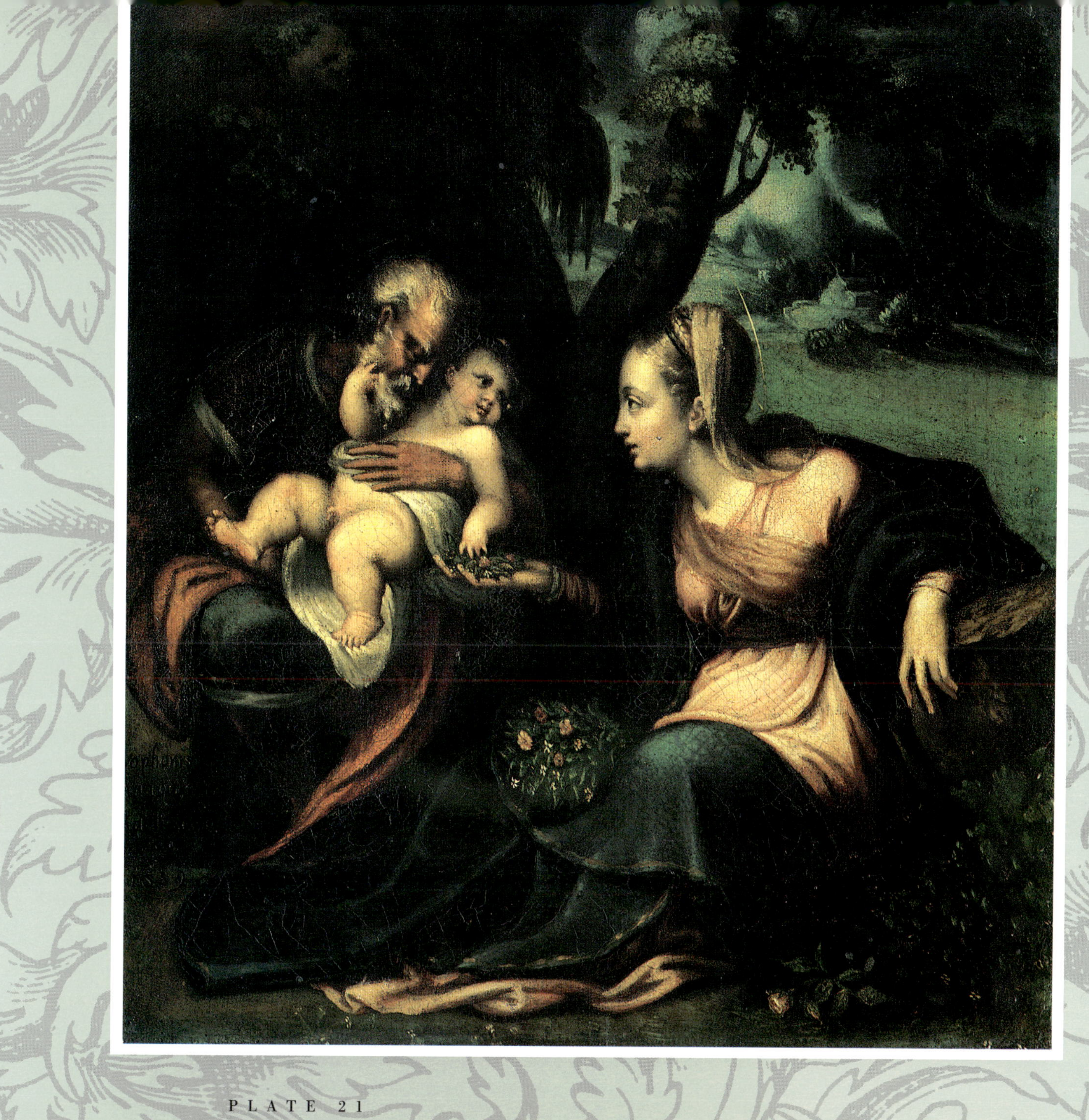

P L A T E 2 1

SOFONISBA ANGUISSOLA

Holy Family

Oil on canvas, 14 1/2 x 12 1/4 in.

Inscribed: SOPHONISBA/ANAGUSSOLA

(sic) ADOLESCENS/P.1559

Bergamo, Accademia Carrara,

inv. no. 982/605

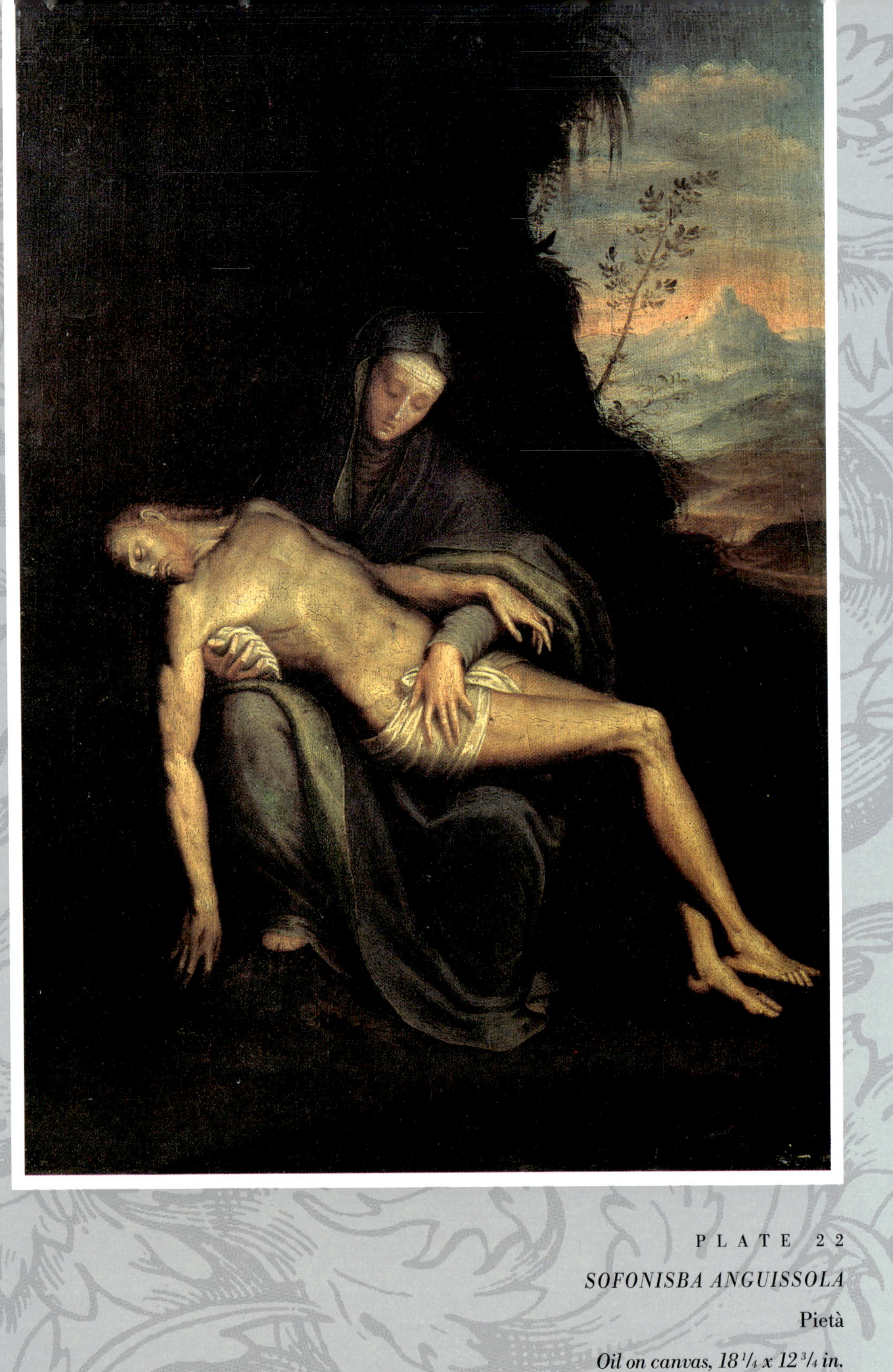

PLATE 22

SOFONISBA ANGUISSOLA

Pietà

Oil on canvas, 18 1/4 x 12 3/4 in.

Milan, Pinacoteca di Brera,

inv. no. 762

This painting has belonged to the Brera in Milan since 1909, and was attributed until 1932 to Bernardino Campi. It has since been assigned to his student Sofonisba, an attribution that research has continued to accept until quite recently. It has been dated about 1550, which is not easily proven. The small painting seems to be based on the central group in Bernardino Campi's large *Pietà* from Santa Caterina in Crema, today also at the Brera (Miller in exh. cat. Cremona 1985, 167). Since their altarpiece was not completed until 1574, Sofonisba, if she were the artist, would have to have made her small copy after an earlier version (so far unknown) of Campi's *Pietà* in Spain. Otherwise, the painting must have been done following her return from Spain, after 1573, in Genoa, Cremona or Sicily. The possibility cannot be ruled out, however, that this is a small-size copy by Campi himself.

Adolfo Venturi analyzed in his *Storia dell'Arte Italiana* (1933, 924) the differences between the two artists with the help of the *Pietà,* which led him and later advocates to plead for an attribution to Sofonisba: "the copy after the work of the master (Bernardino Campi) is scrupulous and true, but it seems as though Sofonisba was more influenced by Parmigianino than her teacher . . . in that the fingers of the Madonna seem like they are polished, in her use of silvery tones, the delicacy of the gently pointed face, the brevity of her brushstrokes. Everything is much lovelier and sweeter." The gentle, spiritual intimacy of the *Pietà* may also evoke the memory of the painting style of Sofonisba's second teacher, Bernardino Gatti, who, in turn, was inspired by Correggio.

In any event, for the moment the attribution, as well as a definite date, must remain open.

Exh. cat. Cremona 1994, no. 34 (V. Guazzoni)

—*WOLFGANG PROHASKA*

PLATE • 22

Genoese Republic's galley, which traversed between Corsica, Nice, Livorno, Naples and Sicily, was given the order to take the Genoese gentlemen to Savona. Sofonisba could not have pass up this opportunity to travel to Savona on her husband's ship, to meet her infanta and several ladies she still knew from the Spanish days. The infanta received the Genoese delegation so majestically that they were all very impressed, and Sofonisba must have felt transported back to old times. Despite her delight, though, she must have relished her current freedom.

The sketches for her *Infanta Catalina Micaela* (plate 19) must have been made in Savona, unless Sofonisba accompanied the infanta to Turin immediately. At the fist opportunity the work must have been sent to Philip II, in gratitude for his recently demonstrated kindness to the artist. This portrait of the infanta is the most beautiful one of her in existence. Sofonisba here demonstrates the maturity she has achieved in her art. The pattern adheres to the regulations of Spanish court portraits. The coloration is similar to other court portraits by Sofonisba and yet, in comparison with the portraits of the mother, Isabel of Valois, this work shows a harmony, finesse and confidence that those portraits do not have. In this portrait Sofonisba demonstrates a freedom in technique that rises far above the severity of the court restrictions. The meeting with the infanta would be followed by others, which, in turn, resulted in more portraits.

One occurrence in the fall of 1585, however, shook the life of the Lomellini family temporarily and showed that, also in Genoa, not everything in Sofonisba's life was defined by art. Orazio Lomellini had chased a pirate ship along the coast of Corsica with the galley belonging to the government of Genoa. Whether due to inexcusable damage to the galley or the cargo, or whether because the risks taken by their war-happy captain seemed too great to the noble gentlemen, Orazio lost his post. From that point onward he would sail only on the Genoa-Sicily route on private merchant ships. This incident demonstrates that the dangers of the sea, which had affected Sofonisba once with the death of Don Fabrizio, periodically unsettled her peaceful, artistic life in Genoa—every time Orazio left for a voyage, in fact. It also indicates that the economic risks associated with her husband's profession were considerable.

Sofonisba visited the Infanta Catalina Micaela later in Turin, at that merry court where the Italian, Spanish and French culture had merged to form a happy union. Evidence of this visit is a second Infanta Catalina Micaela (Glasgow, Pollok House Museum and Art Galleries), which is like an enlarged miniature, showing the infanta in everyday dress. Here the restrictions of the formal portrait have been completely abandoned. The young woman glances quickly at the painter, her expression caught in the picture. The slender, aristocratic, yet highly vibrant, face is exemplary of the height of Sofonisba's ability as a portrait painter, revealing the artist's sensitivity and sense of beauty. In comparison with the first portrait of the infanta from 1585, the nearly identical features provide a perfect example of the difference in expression between a court portrait and a painting privately created by Sofonisba. The duke of Savoy appears to have taken this picture to the king on his trip to Spain in 1591.

The artist must have been in Turin a third time around 1595. She painted a *Margaret of Savoy as a Child*[76] (Madrid, private collection), the first daughter of Catalina Micaela, together with her dwarf. This glimpse into a court nursery, in which the little princess and her servant-companion are painted with the same devotion and respect, may be related, looking to Sofonisba's past, to the *Small Noble Boy with His Servant* (Saint Petersburg, The Hermitage) from the last period of Sofonisba's youth in Italy. Looking to the future, it would become a model for *Las Meninas* by Diego Velázquez (Madrid, Museo del Prado) and his portrait of Prince Balthazar Carlos with a dwarf (Boston, Museum of Fine Arts). Sofonisba's Spanish work thereby posthumously received the greatest possible recognition, in a manner which would have pleased her very much.

Sofonisba's stay in Turin was possibly due to Orazio's months-long absence from Genoa. He had made one of his visits to Palermo and was finally able to collect Sofonisba's dowry from her first marriage.

This must have been her last trip to Turin; the infanta died in 1597 during the birth of her tenth child. In 1598 Philip II passed away as well. Of all the people who had been at court at the same time as Sofonisba, only the Infanta Isabel Clara Eugenia remained. In 1599 Sofonisba had the great satisfaction and pleasure to be reunited also with this infanta and former pupil and exchange memories. The chronicler Ribera writes:

When the Infanta, after her marriage to the Archduke Albert, traveled through Genoa, she (Sofonisba) came to call on her, and Her Highness was so happy to see her that she wanted her nearby during the days she was in Genoa, and they spent many hours together in intimate conversation and remembered the experiences they had shared when the Infanta was at a tender age. She (Sofonisba) told the Infanta she would like to paint her portrait; since she would not be able to finish it during her visit, she would send it, as indeed she did. And the Infanta, as a sign of her great affection, gave her a golden chain of exquisite workmanship, decorated with precious jewels.

This missing *Infanta Isabel Clara Eugenia* has recently been discovered (plate 20). From the careful description in Philip II's inventory, it was recognized among the pictures that were returned from Valladolid as the portrait that is listed next to Sofonisba's three-quarter length portrait of the infanta's mother, described as the portrait of Isabel de Valois "with the flea-fur." This portrait of the infanta is one further large-size representational portrait by Sofonisba. It is much more conventional than the Turin portraits and yet, although very similar in pose and accessories, more freely and generously painted than the full-figure portrait of Isabel of Valois in the Alcázar in Madrid, which had been created thirty-eight years earlier. Above all it is apparent here how much softer and more liberated the technique has become, how much more insightfully the personality is rendered. The small pendant of a saint with its simple chain, which seems out of place next to the valuable string of pearls and the splendid outfit, must have been worn by the infanta only in her home environment—again one of Sofonisba's details that transcends protocol.

In 1606 Peter Paul Rubens, who afterward became court painter to Isabel Clara Eugenia, went to Genoa and must have visited the aged artist, who already was losing her eyesight. Rubens was well aware of Sofonisba's work. In 1603 he had copied a number of important portraits in Spain commissioned by the duke of Mantua, among others Sofonisba's full-length *Isabel of Valois*, which served as model for his *Marchesa Brigida Spinola Doria* (Washington, National Gallery of Art). Undoubtedly, he must have admired Sofonisba's paintings at the Spanish court. Among those he would have seen in Valladolid was the portrait of his future patron Isabel Clara Eugenia. Sofonisba's intimate acquaintance with her, the new sovereign of the Netherlands, must have fostered a tie between the artists. Sofonisba must have been able to help Rubens with her connections, since she had generated such interest among the society in Genoa for the art of portraiture. Anthony van Dyck, who later went to see her in Palermo, was also able to make use of this dual Genoese portrait tradition fashioned by Sofonisba and Rubens.

During her marriage to Orazio Lomellini, Sofonisba confronted a number of concerns as well, and was not free of financial worries. As we know, her dowry became available only after fifteen years of marriage, her pension payments were often delayed for various reasons or sometimes not available at all due to other obligations and Orazio's income must have been irregular. The couple, like most of their contemporaries, depended on a moneylender for their cash. Their primary source was a Genoese merchant, Fabrizio Bargagli, who did not have an easy time collecting debts from them.

In her last years in Genoa Sofonisba made sure her affairs were in order. In 1604 she asked Philip III if she might pass on 400 ducats of her first Sicilian pension of 1,000 ducats to an heir of her choice, since she had no children. That request was granted. This sum was probably for Orazio's illegitimate but acknowledged son, Giulio. Sofonisba's relationship with her stepson, who lived in Palermo, must have been very amicable. In fact, she was godmother to his first daughter, who was named after her. In 1606 she asked to be allowed to transfer the pension from Cremona, which had been collected by her brother since her father's death, directly to his name. Never, not even in extreme need, had she touched this money, as she would have been entitled to do. Her sense of obligation to her family was very strong. Asdrubale predeceased her by two years, but the pension remained with her Cremonese family.

The Move to Palermo[77]

Around 1615 the couple changed their place of residence to Palermo. Orazio Lomellini, although probably some years younger than Sofonisba, who was now approaching her eighties, was at an age at which the constant travel between Genoa and Palermo had become too much for him. While pursuing his profession, he also was able to take care of Sofonisba's pensions and his own businesses based in Sicily. The wish not to give up the contact with Palermo must have been the prime factor in choosing that city and not Genoa for retirement.

In Palermo, Orazio played a greater role in society among the large colony of Genoese merchants—at that time about six hundred in number—than he had in his hometown, where he did not hold any public offices. On several occasions he was elected the Genoese representative on the island. In 1624 he received the office of *Maestro Razionale* (chief of the tax department) of the royal patrimony of the kingdom of Sicily. In 1630 he was named senator of the city of Palermo. He was also among the citizens responsible for the building and decoration of the church San Giorgio dei Genovesi, a duty that usually fell to Genoese artists.

Sofonisba seems to have lived the later years of her life to the fullest. Orazio's responsibility for San Giorgio meant that the couple was in touch with many young artists. In her final years she must have stepped in the limelight one last time. In 1623 Emanuele Filiberto of Savoy, third son of the Infanta Catalina, was made viceroy of Sicily. Philip II had declared him Great Prior of the order of Saint John for Castile and León when he was still a child. He later became grand admiral of the Spanish fleet under his cousin Philip III. Raised as a Spaniard and considered part of the Spanish royal family, this young man must have once more aroused an interest in the elderly lady-in-waiting and former teacher of his mother, who had known him as a seven-year-old in Turin.

Before her death Sofonisba had the pleasure of meeting a great master in her field, Anthony van Dyck, who had resided in Genoa since 1621 and must have heard much about her there, as he already had from Rubens. When he was called by Emanuele Filiberto to Palermo in 1624 to paint his portrait (Dulwich, Dulwich College Picture Gallery), he visited Sofonisba. He was very impressed with the old artist, who held his portrait of her very close to her eyes and gave him advice about the placement of light and shadow in portraits to minimize the wrinkles.

Sofonisba Anguissola died in 1625, lovingly cared for by her husband, probably surrounded by the stepson's family and the grandchildren. Orazio had the following inscription carved on her tombstone in San Giorgio:

To his wife Sofonisba, of the Anguissola family, who was one of the world's famous women because of her nobility, her beauty, and her extraordinary natural gifts, and so outstanding in her representation of the human portrait that no one in her time was held in the same esteem, Horazius Lomellinus, in deepest pain, dedicates this final monument to her who, although small for such a woman, is great among mortals.

Sofonisba, Painter and Woman

As Orazio tells posterity, Sofonisba's paintings, in fact, have an extraordinary quality. Together with Moroni, she is among the first Italian painters who specialized in portraits. Sofonisba thereby turned the constraints she was subjected to as a woman—being limited to small-size works, her rather narrow training in scenical design which led to her close copying of religious paintings—into an advantage. The restrictions of the official court portrait did not constrain her work, it encouraged her to concentrate on her real concern, the essence of her subject's personality.

Capturing this essence is more than a painterly goal for Sofonisba. Even when she does not paint her own family, her interpretation is always positive, if not flattering. Her presentation of her subjects is

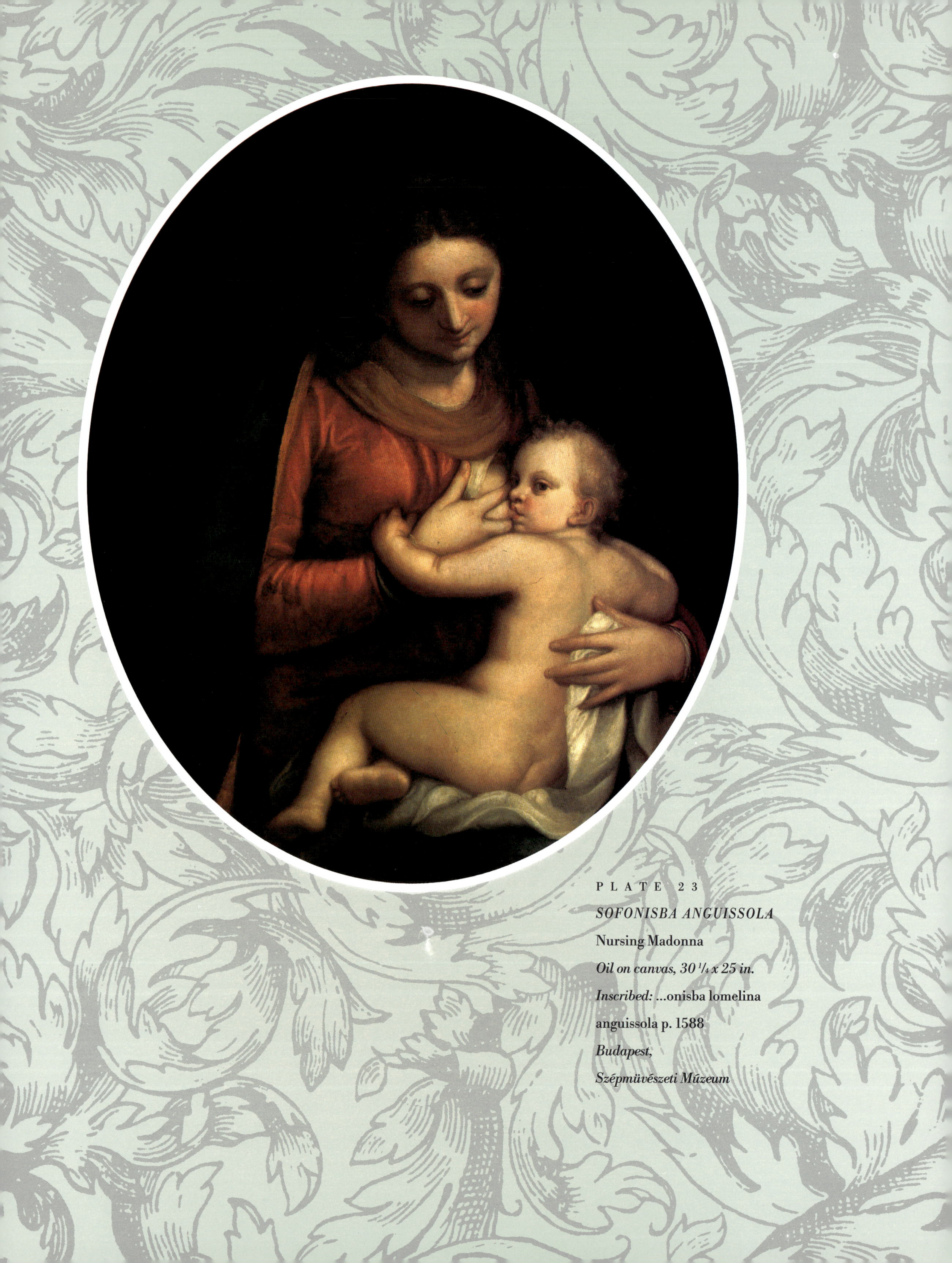

P L A T E 2 3

SOFONISBA ANGUISSOLA

Nursing Madonna

Oil on canvas, 30 1/4 x 25 in.

Inscribed: ...onisba lomelina anguissola p. 1588

Budapest, Szépmüvészeti Múzeum

P L A T E • 2 3

Budapest's Szépmüvészeti Múzeum received this painting as a gift in 1912 from Janos, Count Pálffy, after it had been in the collection of Félicie Dosne, sister-in-law of the French president Adolphe Thiers.

The attribution to Sofonisba seems—without knowledge of a signature—to have been traditionally accepted. Since the 1950s the work had been attributed to Luca Cambiaso and dated just after 1560 (Suida Manning, Suida 1958, 159). Only when the painting was cleaned in 1967 were a signature and date found, and the painting then helped to reconstruct the Genoese period of Sofonisba's life.

Here also, at a comparatively later time, the painter uses the disegno (composition) of another famous painter (compare plates 21, 22 and 24). Sofonisba's model seems to have been a version of Luca Cambiaso's *Madonna del latte,* of which a well-preserved version h as recently appeared on the art market (exh. cat. Cremona 1994, ill. page 266). The date must be the beginning of the 1560s, and the work represents a phase in the evolution of the Genoese artist, which, after a stay in Emilia, is clearly influenced by Correggio. The style must have especially suited the painter—also due to her training. She tries here to emphasize certain traits of Cambiaso, particularly the "sweetness of the Corregesque *Sfumato* after her teacher Bernardino Gatti who always looked to Parma" (Gregori 1985a, 173). Cambiaso himself is always tougher in his treatment of three-dimensionality, harsher in his lighting, the fall of the drapery and the hair.

The example by Cambiaso possibly also points to a later modification to the painting's format in Budapest; it may originally have been rectangular.

Exh. cat. Cremona 1994, no. 35 (R. Sacchi)

—WOLFGANG PROHASKA

P L A T E • 2 4

This last dated work by Sofonisba, which is also the largest one among her narrative paintings, was given to the museum in Florida in 1952 by Mrs. Forbes Hawkes.

The nighttime scene of Anne and the threesome here includes Saint Joseph and Saint John as a child. An impression of familiarity and domesticity has been achieved with the lighting and Anne's occupation with the reel; the boy's tender attention to the grandmother and the mother's to her son; John's inquisitive interest; the curled up dog; and so forth.

There can be no doubt that there existed a prototype of this scene by Cambiaso, although his composition is known only from copies. A further comparison can be made with Cambiaso's *Madonna della candela* of 1570-75 from the Palazzo Bianco in Genoa, which presents a very similar situation with slight variations in the composition. The differences in Sofonisba's own interpretation and her independence are obvious. Where Cambiaso used cold light and stereometric simplification for his Holy Family at the spinning wheel, reflecting the "new objectivity" of the Counter Reformation, Sofonisba envelops the group in warm light and minimizes hard edges and contrasts, reminiscent of both her earlier and later experiments with *sfumato* and the more "endearing" style of Correggio.

Exh. cat. Cremona 1994, no. 36 (R. Sacchi)

—WOLFGANG PROHASKA

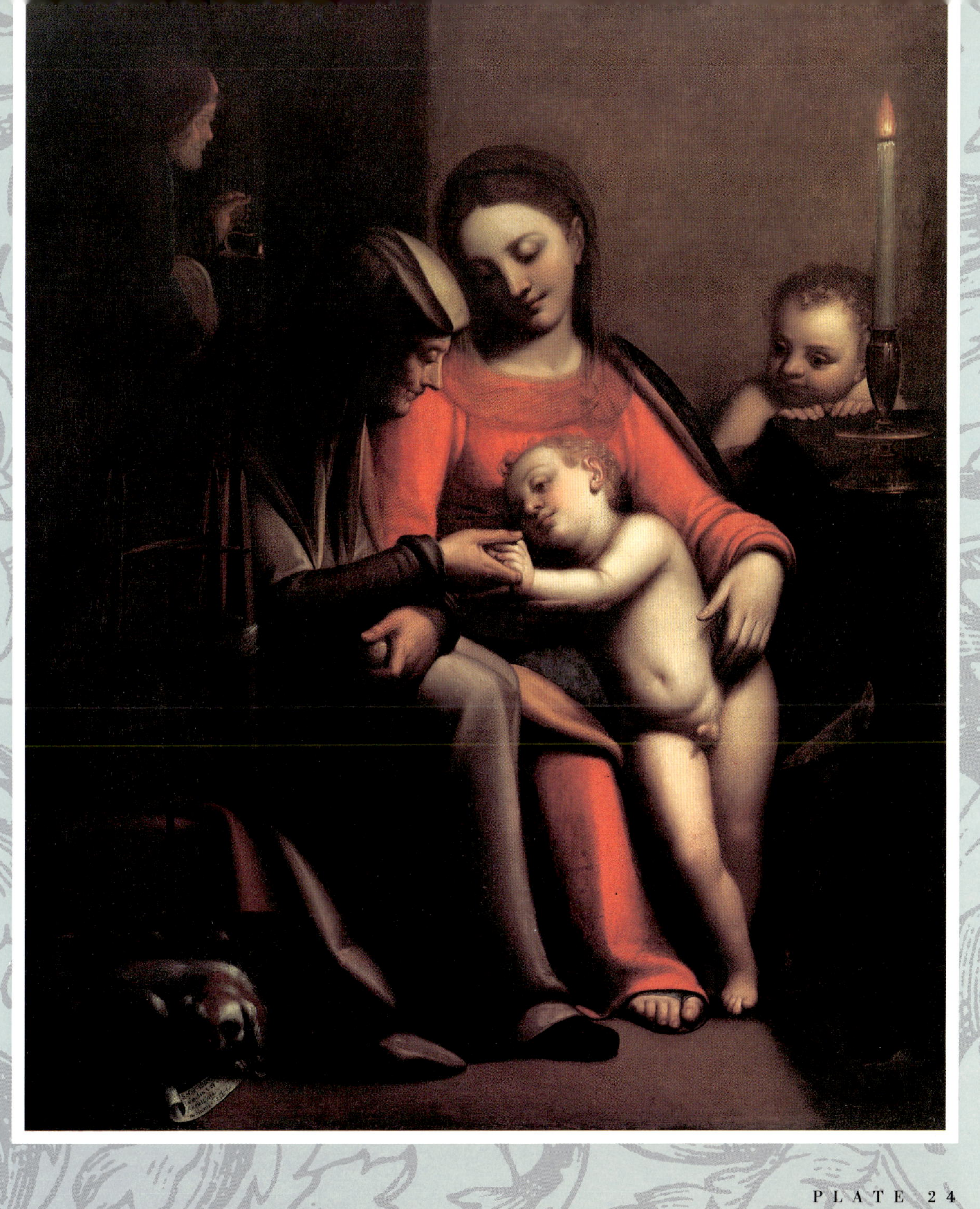

P L A T E 2 4

SOFONISBA ANGUISSOLA

The Holy Family with Saints

Anne and John the Baptist

Oil on canvas, 49 1/2 x 43 1/2 in.

Inscribed: Sofonisba Lomelino

et Anguissola pinsit 1592

Miami, The Lowe Art Museum,

University of Miami

Gift of Mrs. Forbes Hawkes

52.003.000

affectionate, as though she were introducing a good friend to other friends. She searches for the most advantageous light, the best angle, the most agreeable expression, to make visible to the viewer all the beauty and goodness hidden in her model.

In Italy this placed her in a position contrary to pathos and grandeur, and also to the caricaturesque tendencies practiced in her home region, Lombardy. In Spain it distinguished her work from the realism of Alonso Sánchez Coello, the cool dignity of Anthonis Mor and the affected vanity of other court artists. Pathos she countered with unpretentiousness; caricature with humor; stiff formality with naturalness; realism with the greatest possible accentuation of beauty without loss of truth. She explicitly searched for *il vero*, but truth for her was not the same as for her male colleagues. She always looked for the human aspect—in the personalities of her Italian subjects, and later in the king. She saw the child in the infanta and the woman in the queen. She was convinced, however, as were her court subjects themselves, that adherence to certain rules was necessary, although she tried in her portraits to relax them and emphasized the human traits of her subjects. In her portraiture one can always find subtle, covert hints alluding to the situation at hand. She adapts to her surroundings. Her grasp of that which is innately Spanish—the spareness of the medium, the natural dignity of the subject—is striking and led to the inclusion of her work among that of the great Spanish masters.

She takes advantage of Campi's thorough knowledge of drawing and Gatti's finely tuned work after Correggio and his interest in facial features after Leonardo. As a native of Lombardy, she takes joy in dark tonalities, and she has a northern Italian's interest in the depiction of the full-length figure. In Spain she learns from the dignity of Mor; Titian's sublime sense of volume and space; Sánchez Coello's psychological refinement and ingenious variation of color. All of these influences serve to help her painting, yet she distills her very own manner from all these experiences.

In technique, her work is always recognizable from its unequaled combination of miniaturist detail with the fluidity found in the work of Correggio, particularly his shadowing and transitions. The contours of her court subjects are never harsh and severe, as are those of the painters of the Spanish court school, but gently merge with the background of the works. Her figures are never painted in direct, bright light, although Sofonisba loves focused illumination. The freedom, softness and assurance of her technique improves over the years.

From her colorful group portraits in Cremona and the gold-diffused portrait of her mother, Sofonisba, still in Italy, moves on to paint portraits that are restrained in coloration and later become the foundation for her court portraits. She loves certain color combinations which enliven this restraint and make clothing appear especially precious: black against red, gold and yellow; or white against gray and gold. Her counterpoints are small red dots, a precious stone, a ribbon.

Sofonisba's remarkable oeuvre, but also her letters, statements by her contemporaries and bits and pieces assembled from documents, allow us to reconstruct her activities and the events of her life, to lift the veil from the past and participate in her extraordinarily colorful existence. She watches us from her paintings with the bright eyes of the northern Italian; her face, with its glowing skin, is the full oval of women from her region. We know of her humor, warmheartedness and naturalness, her energy and decisiveness, also of her ability to adapt, of her wisdom and her diplomatic skills.

Sofonisba was not just a distinguished painter but also, as Orazio expresses, an eminent and attractive woman. She won the admiration of her male contemporaries and was emulated by women. As a uniquely spellbinding actress on the stage of time, she still moves us today.

NOTES

1. For sources, with a few exceptions, I refer to the notes for essays in the exhibition catalogue *Sofonisba Anguissola e le sue sorelle* (Cremona: Leonardo Arte, 1994), abbreviated here to "Cremona 1994," or to the register of documents and catalogue entries of that publication.

2. In determining Sofonisba's date of birth, her plausible age at the beginning of her apprenticeship with Bernardino Campi in 1546 must be the point of departure. Also the fact that, according to the marriage contract of 1573, she is still expected to be able to have children is significant. Compare Mina Gregori, "Fama e oblio di Sofonisba Anguissola," in Cremona 1994, 18; Rossana Sacchi, "Sofonisba Anguissola," in Cremona 1994, 71. I believe that a date of 1536, or even the later of the dates assumed by Gregori, is probable.

3. Giovanni Vigo, *Cremona nel Cinquecento,* exhibition catalogue (Cremona, 1985), 13. Silvio Leydi, *Cariche e poteri tra Cremona e Milano,* exhibition catalogue (Cremona: Leonardo Arte, 1994), 37-50.

4. Marco Gerolamo Vida, *Cremonensium Orationes III adversus Papienses in controversia Principatus* (Cremona, 1550). About her education and the fostering of women, compare Valerio Guazzoni, "Donna, pittrice e gentildonna: La nascita di un mito femminile del Cinquecento," in Cremona 1994, 57.

5. See note 4.

6. For this and the following essay compare Rossana Sacchi, "Intorno agli Anguissola," in Cremona 1994, 345-50; C. Bonetti, "Nel Centenario di Sofonisba Anguissola," in *Archivio Storico Lombardo* (1928) 55:295.

7. Regarding the names, compare Sacchi, "Intorno agli Anguissola," in Cremona 1994, 345; Ilya Sandra Perlingieri, *Sofonisba Anguissola: The First Great Woman Artist* (New York: Rizzoli, 1992), 27.

8. Regarding the problem of the birthdates, compare Anastasia Gilardi, "Le sorelle di Sofonisba," in Cremona 1994, 75-78.

9. Sacchi, "Intorno agli Anguissola," in Cremona 1994, 345.

10. About this paragraph regarding the education of women and Amilcare's pioneering plan to let the girls apprentice with a painter, see Guazzoni, "Donna, pittrice e gentildonna," in Cremona 1994, 57-70.

11. Compare Guazzoni, "Donna, pittrice e gentildonna," in Cremona 1994, 59. The complete text of the letter can be found in the register of documents in Cremona 1994, 363.

12. Giorgio Vasari, *Le Vite de' più eccellenti pittori, scultori ed architettori* (1568), edition Milanesi (Florence, 1878-85), 6:501.

13. Alessandro Lamo, *Discorso...intorno alla scoltura e pittura...* (1584), in Giovan Battista Zaist (1774), in *Notizie istoriche...di G. B. Zaist* (Cremona, 1976), 1:34-36. Complete text in Cremona 1994, 406-08. In my opinion, this passage by Lamo was taken too literally. Since it is important for the apprenticeship and the motives of Amilcare, I have tried to analyze it more thoroughly.

14. This represents Rossana Sacchi's (verbal communication) and my own opinion, which differs from Guazzoni and Bora. Compare Guazzoni, "Donna, pittrice e gentildonna," in Cremona 1994, 62; Giulio Bora, "Sofonisba Anguissola e la sua formazione cremonese: Il ruolo del disegno," in Cremona 1994, 79.

15. Considering that the art of painting in general was acknowledged in Cremona, this interpretation of Lamos's text seems the only one possible. Amilcare, therefore, was completely aware of the pioneering significance of this step.

16. About the education of the sisters by Bernardino Campi and Bernardino Gatti, compare Bora, "La sua formazione cremonese," in Cremona 1994, 79-88.

17. For the analysis of the origin of Sofonisba's art, I depend on Gregori, "Fama e oblio," in Cremona 1994, 16, about portraiture *dal naturale.*

18. See here also Gregori, "Fama e oblio," in Cremona 1994, 18. The idea that Gatti may have asked Sofonisba's help with sketches for a large composition turns out to be erroneous. The drawings attributed to Sofonisba by Bora, "La sua formazione cremonese," in Cremona 1994, 79-88, are by Fernando Yañez and are preparatory drawings for one of his altars.

19. Vida, *Cremonensium Orationes III*. Complete text and notes in Cremona 1994, 403.

20. Gilardi, "Le sorelle di Sofonisba," in Cremona 1994, 75.

21. *Self-Portrait*, Milan, Castello Sforzesco; *Dr. Pietro Manna*, plate 11; *Bianca Ponzoni*, Rome, Galleria Borghese; *Minerva Anguissola(?)*, Milan, Museo Poldi Pezzoli; *Portrait of Europa*, (plate 12). Compare also Flavio Caroli, "Per Lucia Anguissola," in *Paragone* 277 (1973): 69-73; Gregori, "Fama e oblio," in Cremona 1994, 24; Gilardi, "Le sorelle di Sofonisba," in Cremona 1994, 75.

22. Gilardi, "Le sorelle di Sofonisba," in Cremona 1994, 75.

23. Since the drawing dates earlier than the drawing of the *Boy Bitten by a Crab*, which should be dated 1554/1555 because of Asdrubale's age, in my opinion, the sister cannot be Europa, as Bora believes. Europa is considerably younger in the painting of the sisters playing chess, which is dated 1555. Compare Cremona 1994, cat. no. 37 (Bora).

24. Compare Cremona 1994, cat. no. 39 (de Klerck).

25. Tommaso Cavlieri, letter of 20 January 1562 to Cosimo I de' Medici. Complete text in Cremona 1994, 370.

26. Vasari (1568), edition Milanesi 1881, 5:88.

27. Evident from a letter written by the painter Francesco Salviati to Bernardino Campi from Rome on 28 April 1554. Complete text in Cremona 1994, 408.

28. See Gregori, "Fama e oblio," in Cremona 1994, 23.

29. See Gregori, "Fama e oblio," in Cremona 1994, 16, 20.

30. For the interpretation of the painting, compare Guazzoni, "Donna, pittrice e gentildonna," in Cremona 1994, 57-68, esp. 68.

31. This *Amilcare in His Old Age* with a fur collar, seated in a wing chair, could not be included in the Cremona exhibition due to lack of time. There are parallels in this work to the *Minerva Anguissola* (plate 13). I believe that both works, with their poster-like, composition and simpler technique, are by Europa.

32. See Cremona 1994, cat. no. 2 (Sacchi).

33. Letter of 1 February 1556, printed in its entirety in Cremona 1994, 363.

34. A. Luzio, La Galleria dei Gonzaga, venduta all'Inghilterra nel 1627-1628. Documenti degli Archivi di Mantova e Londra, Milan 1913.

35. See Cremona 1994, cat. no. 5 (Sacchi).

36. Compare Cremona 1994, 25, plate 1, text cat. no. 6 (Sacchi).

37. Complete text of the letters written by Annibale Caro on 23 December 1558 and 14 July 1559, in Cremona 1994, 365.

38. Compare Kusche, "Il ritratto di rappresentanza ufficiale," in Cremona 1994, 125.

39. See Gregori, "Fama e oblio," in Cremona 1994, 19.

40. Compare Cremona 1994, cat. no. 17 (Sacchi).

41. Compare Cremona 1994, cat. no. 39 (de Klerck). For the complete text of the letter by Tommaso Cavalieri to Cosimo I de' Medici of 20 January 1562, and an accompanying letter to the drawing by Averardo Serristori of 24 January, see Cremona 1994, 370.

42. For the complete text of the letters of 7 May 1557 and 15 May 1558, from Amilcare to Michelangelo, see Cremona 1994, 364-65.

43. Gregori, "Fama e oblio," in Cremona 1994, 24; Cremona 1994, cat. nos. 32, 34 (Guazzoni).

44. See the detailed description of the activities of Irene di Spilimbergo. She was a student of Titian, only slightly younger than Sofonisba, and emulated her work. Compare Guazzoni, "Donna, pittrice e gentildonna," in Cremona 1994, 65.

45. Michela Mazzolaro and Giulia Rigoni Savioli, *La condizione femminile*, exhibition catalogue (Cremona: Leonardo Arte, 1994), 106.

46. Sacchi, "Intorno agli Anguissola," in Cremona 1994, 351.

47. For this paragraph, I refer to Kusche, "Al servizio dei re di Spagna," in Cremona 1994, 89-93, and Kusche, "Il ritratto di rappresentanza ufficiale," in Cremona 1994, 138, 145. I also refer to the sources mentioned there.

48. Antonio Campo, *Cremona Fidelissima Città* (Cremona, 1585), X.

49. Campo, *Cremona Fidelissima*, XXX.

50. Complete text and notes in Cremona 1994, 366.

51. Pietro Paolo de Ribera, *Le Glorie immortali de' Trionfi, et Heroiche Imprese di Ottocento Quarantacinque Donne Illustri antiche e moderne...* (Venice, 1609), 313-16. All other biographers of Sofonisba copy from him.

52. Complete text and notes in Cremona 1994, 366.

53. After comparing the works in the exhibition directly with Sofonisba's self-portraits, they seem to me rather made by Lucia, who could have painted her sister in Milan. The portrait from Brescia by Sofonisba's hand, in Cremona 1994, cat. no. 21 (Sacchi–the catalogue entry in the first edition is attributed to me in error), however, seems to represent her sister Lucia. It has the same slanted eyes as in Lucia's *Self-Portrait*, cat. no. 42, and as in Lucia's image in *The Chess Game* (plate 6).

54. Giovanni Paolo Lomazzo, *Gli sogni e raggionamenti composti da Giovan Paolo Lomazzo milanese* (1563/1564), edition R. P. Ciardi, 1973, 95. Complete text in Cremona 1994, 404.

55. This paragraph is based on Kusche, "Al servizio dei re di Spagna," in Cremona 1994, 89-100, and Kusche, "Il ritratto di rappresentanza ufficiale," in Cremona 1994, 126-34. It also refers to the sources listed there.

56. Complete text and notes in Cremona 1994, 367.
57. For complete text and notes see Kusche, "Al servizio dei re di Spagna," in Cremona 1994, 93.

58. For complete text and notes see Kusche, "Al servizio dei re di Spagna," in Cremona 1994, 93.

59. Ribera, *Le Glorie immortali de' Trionfi*, 313.

60. For the letter to Bernardino Campi of 21 October, see notes in Cremona 1994, 369.

61. This paragraph is based Kusche, "Al servizio dei re di Spagna," in Cremona 1994, 100-05, and Kusche, "Il ritratto di rappresentanza uffiziale," in Cremona 1994, 134-37. It also refers to the sources listed there.

62. Complete text and notes in Cremona 1994, 373-74.

63. Complete text in Cremona 1994, 378.

64. Text and notes in Cremona 1994, 379.

65. For Sofonisba's life in Palermo I refer to Rossana Sacchi, "Tra la Sicilia e Genova: Sofonisba Anguissola Moncada e poi Lomellini," in Cremona 1994, 153-59. Regarding the relationship to the king, see Kusche, "Al servizio dei re di Spagna," and the sources listed there.

66. Text and notes in Cremona 1994, 379.

67. Ribera, *Le Glorie immortali de' Trionfi*, 315.

68. Memorandum of 27 April 1573, and letter of 15 May (mailed on 12 June) with complete text in Cremona 1994, 382-83. Regarding these events see also Kusche, "Al servizio dei re di Spagna," in Cremona 1994, 106.

69. This part is based on Kusche, "Al servizio dei re di Spagna," in Cremona 1994, 108-11, and the sources listed there.

70. R. Soprani, *La vite de' pittori, scoltori et architetti genovesi e de' forastieri che in Genova operarono con alucuni rittrati de gli stessi* (1674), edition Ratti 1768-69, 415.

71. Complete text and notes in Cremona 1994, 385.

72. Complete text and notes in Cremona 1994, 385.

73. The comments about the financial situation of the Lomellini and the description of Sofonisba's social life, as well as her artistic contacts, are based on the essay by Sacchi, "Tra la Sicilia e Genova," in Cremona 1994, 159-68. For the relationship with Spain and the royal family, their portraits and Rubens, see Kusche, "Al servizio dei re di Spagna," in Cremona 1994, 110-13, and Kusche, "Il rittrato di rappresentanza ufficiale," in Cremona 1994, 140-50, and the sources listed there.

74. Complete text and notes in Cremona 1994, 387.

75. Complete text and notes in Cremona 1994, 408.

76. Compare with the portrait of Margaret of Savoy by Frans Pourbus in San Carlo al Corso, Rome. Illustrated in *Mostra Iconografica Gonzaghesca*, exhibition catalogue (Mantua, 1937), unnumbered.

77. For this paragraph I rely entirely on Sacchi, "Tra la Sicilia e Genova," in Cremona 1994, 168-70, and refer to the sources listed there.

Exhibition Catalogue Madrid 1963: *Museo del Prado. Catálogo de las pinturas,* ed F. J. Sanchez Cantón. Madrid: Museo del Prado, 1963.

Exhibition Catalogue Cremona 1985: *I Campi e la cultura artistica cremonese del Cinquecento,* ed. Mina Gregori. Milan: Electa, 1985.

Exhibition Catalogue Madrid 1990: *Alonso Sánchez Coello y el retrato en la corte de Felipe II,* ed. Santiago Saavedra. Madrid: Museo del Prado, 1990.

Exhibition Catalogue Bologna 1994: *Lavinia Fontana 1552-1614,* ed. Vera Fortunati. Milan: Electa, 1994.

Exhibition Catalogue Cremona 1994: *Sofonisba Anguissola e le sue sorelle,* ed. Paolo Buffa. Milan: Leonardo Arte, 1994.

Exhibition Catalogue Vienna 1995: *Sofonisba Anguissola: Die Malerin der Renaissance,* ed. Sylvia Ferino-Pagden. Vienna: Kunsthistorisches Museum, 1995.

Berenson, Bernard. *Italian Pictures of the Renaissance. Central Italian and North Italian Schools,* third edition. London: Phaidon 1968.

_____. *The Italian Painters of the Renaissance. Vol. 1, The Venetian Painters.* The North Italian Painters. New York: Phaidon, 1968.

Breuer, Stephanie. *Alonso Sánchez Coello.* Ph.D. diss. Munich, 1984.

_____. "Alonso Sánchez Coello vida y obra." In *Alonso Sánchez Coello y el retrato en la corte de Felipe II,* 14-35. Madrid: Museo del Prado, 1990.

Caroli, Flavio. "Per Lucia Anguissola." *Paragone,* 277 (1973): 69-73.

_____. *Sofonisba Anguissola e le sue sorelle.* Milan, 1987.

de Tolnay, Charles. "Sofonisba Anguissola and Her Relations with Michelangelo." *Journal of the Walters Art Gallery* 4 (1941): 115-19.

di Giampaolo, Mario. "Camillo Boccaccino: A Painting and a Drawing." *Burlington Magazine* 120, no. 899 (1978): 82-85.

Fernández Gimenez, E. *Guide to the Permanent Collection.* Milwaukee: Milwaukee Art Museum, 1986.

Ferino-Pagden, Sylvia. *Sofonisba Anguissola: Die Malerin der Renaissance.* Vienna: Kunsthistorisches Museum, 1995.

Garrido, Carmen. "Estudio técnico." In *Alonso Sánchez Coello y el retrato en la corte de Felipe II,* 215-43. Madrid: Museo del Prado, 1990.

Ghirardi, Angela. "Una ricerca iconografica nel cenacolo delle Anguissola: In ritratti di Minerva." *Paragone* 509-11 (1992): 35-43.

_____. "Lavinia Fontana allo specchio: Pittrici e autoritratto nel secondo Cinquecento." In *Lavinia Fontana 1552-1614,* 37-51. Milan: Electa 1994.

Gilardi, Anastasia. "Le sorelle di Sofonisba." In *Sofonisba Anguissola e le sue sorelle,* 75-78. Cremona: Leonardo Arte, 1994.

Giononi-Visani and Gamulin. *Giulio Clovio.* Zagreb, 1993.

Gregori, Mina. "Fama e oblio di Sofonisba Anguissola." In *Sofonisba Anguissola e le sue sorelle,* 11-47. Cremona: Leonardo Arte, 1994.

_____. "Sofonisba Anguissola." In *I Campi e la cultura artistica cremonese del Cinquecento,* 171-178. Milan: Electa, 1985.

Guazzoni, Valerio. "Donna, pittrice e gentildonna: La nascita di un mito femminile del Cinquecento." In *Sofonisba Anguissola e le sue sorelle,* 57-70. Milan: Leonardo Arts, 1994.

Kusche, Maria. *Juan Pantoja de la Cruz,* Madrid, 1964.

_____. "Sofonisba Anguissola en España, retratista en la corte de Felipe II junto a Alonso Sánchez Coello y Jorge de la Rua." *Archivo Español de Arte* 62, no. 248 (1989): 391-420.

Kusche 1991a: Kusche, Maria. "La Antigua Galería de Retratos del Pardo I: Su reconstrucción arquitectónica y el orden de colocación de los cuadros." *Archivo Español de Arte* 64, no. 253 (1991): 1-28.

Kusche 1991b: Kusche, Maria. "La Antigua Galería de Retratos del Pardo II: Su reconstrucción pictórica." *Archivo Español de Arte* 64, no. 255 (1991): 261-81.

Kusche 1991c: Kusche, Maria. "Der christliche Ritter und seine Dame. Das Repräsentationsbildnis in ganzer Figur." *Pantheon* 49 (1991): 4-35.

Kusche 1992a: Kusche, Maria. "Sofonisba Anguissola, Retratista de la Corte Española." *Paragone* 509-11 (1992): 3-34.

Kusche 1992b: Kusche, Maria. "Sofonisba Anguissola. Vuelta a Italia. Continuación de sus relaciones con la corte española." *Paragone* 513 (1992): 10-35.

Kusche 1992c: Kusche, Maria. "La Antigua Galería de Retratos del Pardo III: Su importancia para la obra de Tiziano, Moro, Sánchez Coello y Sofonisba Anguissola y su significado para Felipe II, su fundador." *Archivo Español de Arte* 65, no. 257 (1992): 1-36.

Kusche 1994: Kusche, Maria. "Sofonisba e il ritratto di rappresentanza ufficiale nella corte spagnola." In *Sofonisba Anguissola e le sue sorelle*, 117-152. Milan: Leonardo Arte, 1994.

Kusche 1995: Kusche, Maria. "Sofonisba Anguissola–Leben Und Werk." In *Sofonisba Anguissola: Die Malerin der Renaissance*, ed. Sylvia Ferino-Pagden, 23-57. Vienna: Kunsthistorisches Museum, 1995.

Meloni-Trkulja, Silvia. *Omaggio a Leopoldo de' Medici, parte II, i ritrattini.* Florence: L. S. Olschki, 1976.

Miller, Robert. "Bernardino Campi." In *I Campi e la cultura artistica cremonese del Cinquecento*, 154-70. Milan: Electa, 1985.

Odorici, Federico. *Guida di Brescia, in rapporto alle arti ed ai monumenti antichi e moderni.* Brescia: Tip Giberti, 1853.

Rodeschini-Galati, Maria Christina. "Sofonisba Anguissola, Lucia Anguissola." In *La pittura a Cremona dal Romanico al Settecento*, 271-75. Cinisello Balsamo, 1990.

Rossi, Francesco."Medaglie." In *I Campi e la cultura artistica cremonese del Cinquecento*, 347-68. Milan: Electa, 1985.

Rossi, Ottavio. *Elogi historici di Bresciani illustri.* Brescia: B. Fontana, 1620.

Sacchi, Federico. *Notizie Pittoriche cremonesi.* Cremona, 1872.

Sambo, Elisabetta. "Schede." In *I Campi e la cultura artistica cremonese del Cinquecento.* Milan: Electa, 1985.

Schweikart, Gunter. "Boccaccios 'De claris mulierbus' und die Selbstdarstellung von Malerinnen im 16 Jahrhundert." *Der Künstler über sich selbst in seinem Werk* (1989), reprint (1992).

Simon, Robert B. "The Identity of Sofonisba Anguissola's Young Man." *Journal of the Walters Art Gallery* 44 (1986): 117-22.

Suida, Bertina Manning, and William Suida. *Luca Cambiaso. La vita, le opere.* Milan: Ceschina, 1958.

Venturi, Adolfo. *Storia dell'Arte Italiana* vol. 9, part 6. Milan, 1933.

Wey, Francis Alphonse. *Les Anglais chez eux.* 1861. Reprint. London: Sidwick and Jackson, 1935.

EXHIBITION *Checklist*

SOFONISBA ANGUISSOLA
The Artist's Sister in the Garb of a Nun
Oil on canvas, 29 1/2 x 23 1/4 in.
Collection Southampton City Art Gallery

SOFONISBA ANGUISSOLA
Self-Portrait
Oil on panel, 6 3/4 x 4 3/4 in.
Collection Kunsthistorisches Museum

SOFONISBA ANGUISSOLA
Self-Portrait [in Miniature]
Oil on parchment, 3 1/4 x 2 1/2 in.
Collection Museum of Fine Arts, Boston

SOFONISBA ANGUISSOLA
Self-Portrait at the Easel
Oil on canvas, 26 x 22 1/2 in.
Collection Muzeum Zamek

COPY AFTER SOFONISBA ANGUISSOLA
Self-Portrait at the Spinet
Oil on canvas, 42 1/2 x 42 1/8 in.
Collection Goodwood House

SOFONISBA ANGUISSOLA
The Chess Game
Oil on canvas, 28 3/8 x 38 1/8 in.
Collection Muzeum Narodowe

SOFONISBA ANGUISSOLA
Massimiliano Stampa
Oil on canvas, 54 x 28 1/8 in.
Collection The Walters Art Gallery

SOFONISBA ANGUISSOLA
Portrait of a Monk
Oil on canvas, 22 1/2 x 20 7/8 in.
Collection Pinacoteca Tosio Martinengo

SOFONISBA ANGUISSOLA
Giulio Clovio
Oil on canvas, 39 3/8 x 29 3/4 in.
Collection Federico Zeri

SOFONISBA ANGUISSOLA
Self-Portrait [Round]
Oil on walnut, diameter 4 in.
Collection Galleria degli Uffizi

LUCIA ANGUISSOLA
Dr. Pietro Manna
Oil on canvas, 37 1/2 x 30 in.
Collection Museo del Prado

LUCIA ANGUISSOLA
Europa Anguissola
Oil on panel, diameter ca. 5 3/4 in.
Collection Pinacoteca Tosio Martinengo

EUROPA ANGUISSOLA(?)
Minerva Anguissola
Oil on canvas, 33 1/2 x 26 in.
Collection Milwaukee Art Museum

JUAN PANTOJA DE LA CRUZ(?) AFTER SOFONISBA ANGUISSOLA
(Valladolid 1554-Madrid 1608)
Isabel of Valois
Oil on canvas, 47 x 33 in.
Collection Museo del Prado

SOFONISBA ANGUISSOLA
Isabel of Valois
Oil on canvas, 80 3/4 x 48 1/2 in.
Collection Museo del Prado

SOFONISBA ANGUISSOLA
Isabel of Valois
Oil on canvas, 26 7/8 x 21 3/8 in.
Collection Kunsthistorisches Museum

SOFONISBA ANGUISSOLA
Philip II
Oil on canvas, 34 5/8 x 28 3/8 in.
Collection Museo del Prado

SOFONISBA ANGUISSOLA
Anne of Austria
Oil on canvas, 33 x 26 3/8 in.
Collection Museo del Prado

SOFONISBA ANGUISSOLA
Infanta Catalina Micaela
Oil on canvas, 43 3/4 x 35 7/8 in.
Collection Museo del Prado

SOFONISBA ANGUISSOLA
Infanta Isabel Clara Eugenia
Oil on canvas, 76 5/8 x 43 1/4 in.
Collection Museo del Prado

SOFONISBA ANGUISSOLA
Holy Family
Oil on canvas, 14 1/2 x 12 1/4 in.
Collection Accademia Carrara

SOFONISBA ANGUISSOLA
Pietà
Oil on canvas, 18 1/4 x 12 3/4 in.
Collection Pinacoteca di Brera

SOFONISBA ANGUISSOLA
Nursing Madonna
Oil on canvas, 30 1/4 x 25 in.
Collection Szépmüvészeti Múzeum

SOFONISBA ANGUISSOLA
The Holy Family with Saints Anne and John the Baptist
Oil on canvas, 49 1/2 x 43 1/2 in.
Collection The Lowe Art Museum, University of Miami
Gift of Mrs. Forbes Hawkes